COLLECTION EDITOR: **JENNIFER GRÜNWALD**
ASSISTANT EDITOR: **SARAH BRUNSTAD**
ASSOCIATE MANAGING EDITOR: **ALEX STARBUCK**
EDITOR, SPECIAL PROJECTS: **MARK D. BEAZLEY**
SENIOR EDITOR, SPECIAL PROJECTS: **JEFF YOUNGQUIST**
SVP PRINT, SALES & MARKETING: **DAVID GABRIEL**

EDITOR IN CHIEF: **AXEL ALONSO**
CHIEF CREATIVE OFFICER: **JOE QUESADA**
PUBLISHER: **DAN BUCKLEY**
EXECUTIVE PRODUCER: **ALAN FINE**

AVENGERS VOL. 6: INFINITE AVENGERS. Contains material originally published in magazine form as AVENGERS #29-34. First printing 2014. ISBN# 978-0-7851-5478-5. Published by MARVEL WORLDWIDE, INC., subsidiary of MARVEL ENTERTAINMENT, LLC. OFFICE OF PUBLICATION: 135 West 50th Street, New York, NY 10020. Copyright © 2014 Marvel Characters, Inc. All rights reserved. All characters featured in this issue and t distinctive names and likenesses thereof, and all related indicia are trademarks of Marvel Characters, Inc. No similarity between any of the names, characters, persons, and/or institutions in this magazine with those of a living or dead person or institution is intended, and any such similarity which may exist is purely coincidental. **Printed in the U.S.A.** ALAN FINE, EVP - Office of the President, Marvel Worldwide, Inc. and EVP & CMO Marv Characters B.V.; DAN BUCKLEY, Publisher & President - Print, Animation & Digital Divisions; JOE QUESADA, Chief Creative Officer; TOM BREVOORT, SVP of Publishing; DAVID BOGART, SVP of Operations & Procuremen Publishing; C.B. CEBULSKI, SVP of Creator & Content Development; DAVID GABRIEL, SVP Print, Sales & Marketing; JIM O'KEEFE, VP of Operations & Logistics; DAN CARR, Executive Director of Publishing Technology; SUS CRESPI, Editorial Operations Manager; ALEX MORALES, Publishing Operations Manager; STAN LEE, Chairman Emeritus. For information regarding advertising in Marvel Comics or on Marvel.com, please contact Niza Dis Director of Marvel Partnerships, at ndisla@marvel.com. For Marvel subscription inquiries, please call 800-217-9158. **Manufactured between 9/5/2014 and 10/20/2014 by R.R. DONNELLEY, INC., SALEM, VA, USA.**

10 9 8 7 6 5 4 3 2 1

AVENGERS

WRITER: **JONATHAN HICKMAN**

PENCILER: **LEINIL FRANCIS YU**

INKER: **GERRY ALANGUILAN**

COLORISTS: **SUNNY GHO** WITH **MATT MILLA** [ISSUE 34]

LETTERERS: **VC'S CORY PETIT** [ISSUES 29-31, 33-34] AND
CLAYTON COWLES [ISSUE 32]

COVER ART: **FRANK CHO & JASON KEITH** [ISSUE 29] AND
LEINIL FRANCIS YU & SUNNY GHO [ISSUES 30-34]

ASSISTANT EDITOR: **JAKE THOMAS**

EDITORS: **TOM BREVOORT** WITH **WIL MOSS**

PREVIOUSLY IN AVENGERS

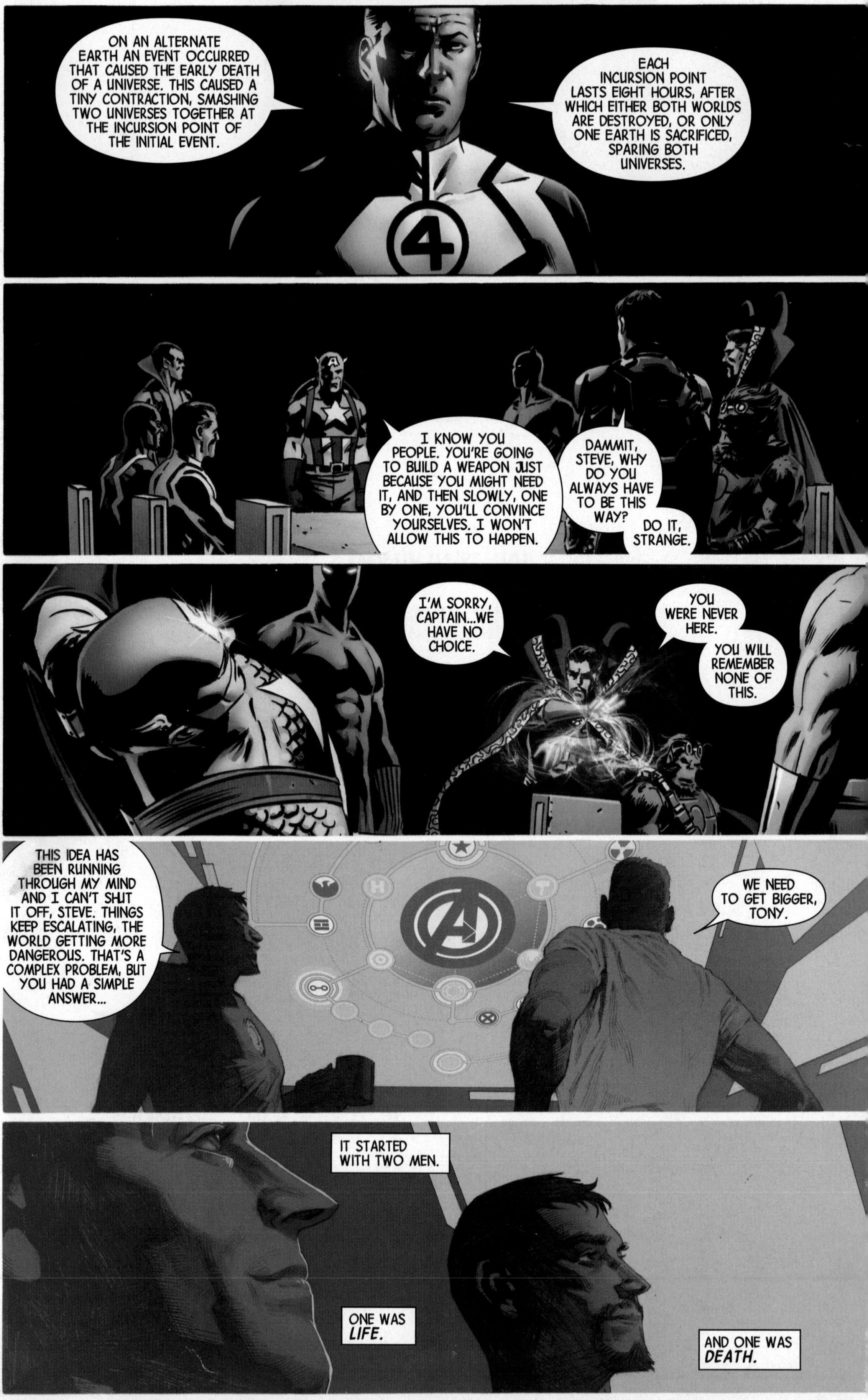
ON AN ALTERNATE EARTH AN EVENT OCCURRED THAT CAUSED THE EARLY DEATH OF A UNIVERSE. THIS CAUSED A TINY CONTRACTION, SMASHING TWO UNIVERSES TOGETHER AT THE INCURSION POINT OF THE INITIAL EVENT.
EACH INCURSION POINT LASTS EIGHT HOURS, AFTER WHICH EITHER BOTH WORLDS ARE DESTROYED, OR ONLY ONE EARTH IS SACRIFICED, SPARING BOTH UNIVERSES.
I KNOW YOU PEOPLE. YOU'RE GOING TO BUILD A WEAPON JUST BECAUSE YOU MIGHT NEED IT, AND THEN SLOWLY, ONE BY ONE, YOU'LL CONVINCE YOURSELVES. I WON'T ALLOW THIS TO HAPPEN.
DAMMIT, STEVE, WHY DO YOU ALWAYS HAVE TO BE THIS WAY?
DO IT, STRANGE.
I'M SORRY, CAPTAIN...WE HAVE NO CHOICE.
YOU WERE NEVER HERE.
YOU WILL REMEMBER NONE OF THIS.
THIS IDEA HAS BEEN RUNNING THROUGH MY MIND AND I CAN'T SHUT IT OFF, STEVE. THINGS KEEP ESCALATING, THE WORLD GETTING MORE DANGEROUS. THAT'S A COMPLEX PROBLEM, BUT YOU HAD A SIMPLE ANSWER...
WE NEED TO GET BIGGER, TONY.
IT STARTED WITH TWO MEN.
ONE WAS *LIFE.*
AND ONE WAS *DEATH.*

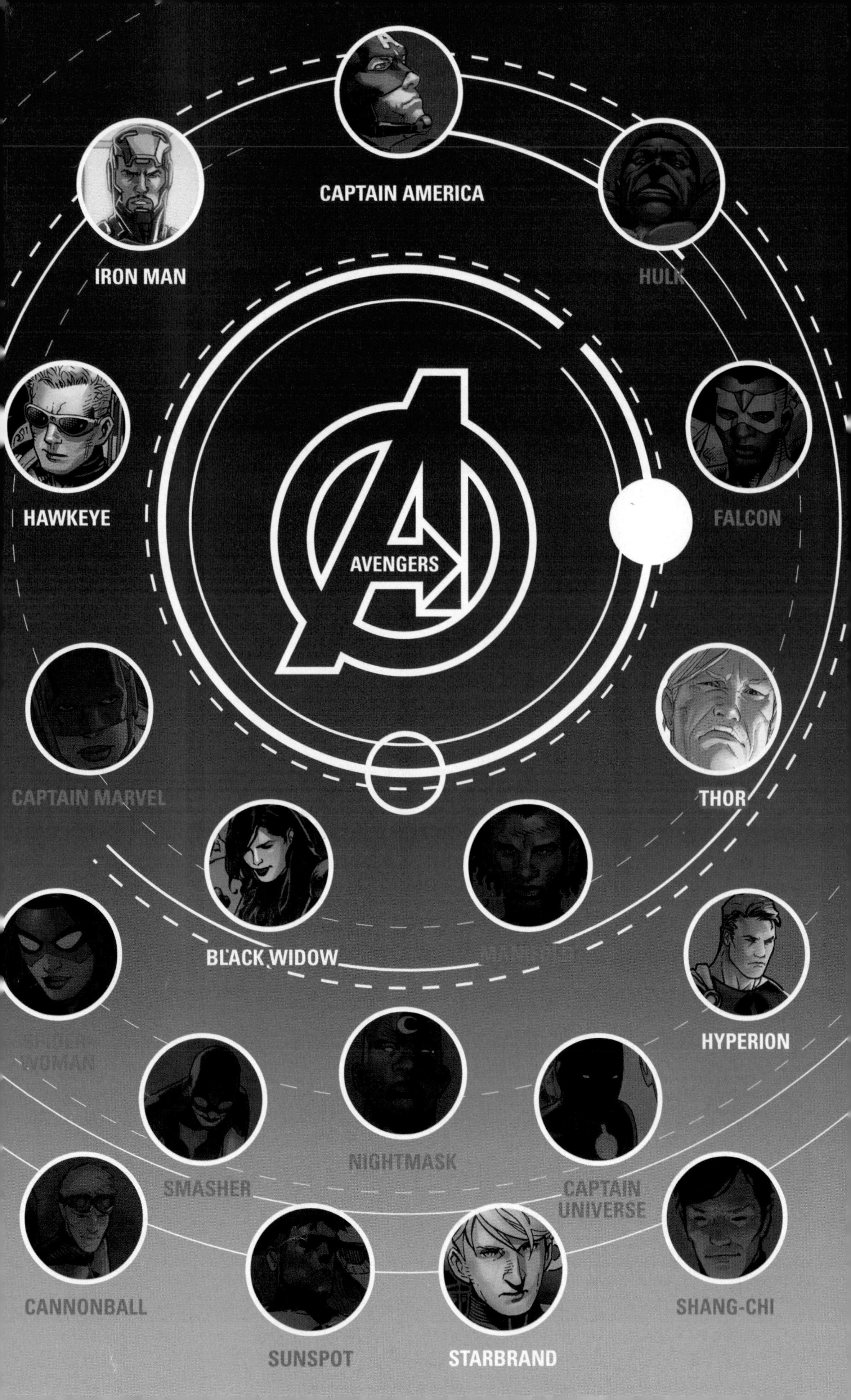
CAPTAIN AMERICA
IRON MAN
HULK
HAWKEYE
AVENGERS
FALCON
CAPTAIN MARVEL
THOR
BLACK WIDOW
SPIDER-
WOMAN
HYPERION
NIGHTMASK
SMASHER
CAPTAIN
UNIVERSE
CANNONBALL
SHANG-CHI
SUNSPOT
STARBRAND

"INFINITE AVENGERS"

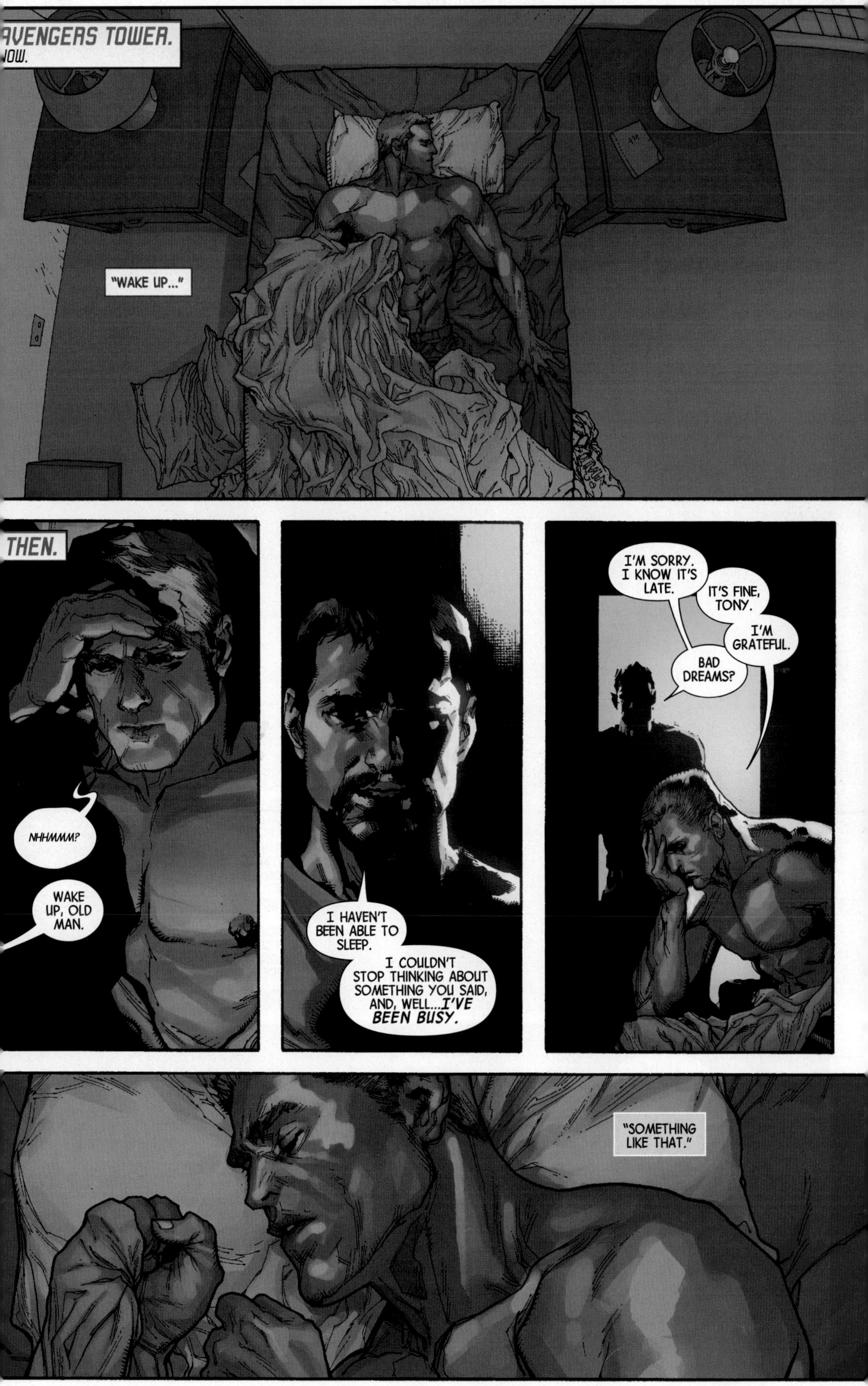
AVENGERS TOWER.
NOW.
"WAKE UP..."
THEN.
NHHMMM?
WAKE UP, OLD MAN.
I HAVEN'T BEEN ABLE TO SLEEP.
I COULDN'T STOP THINKING ABOUT SOMETHING YOU SAID, AND, WELL...I'VE BEEN BUSY.
I'M SORRY. I KNOW IT'S LATE.
IT'S FINE, TONY.
I'M GRATEFUL.
BAD DREAMS?
"SOMETHING LIKE THAT."

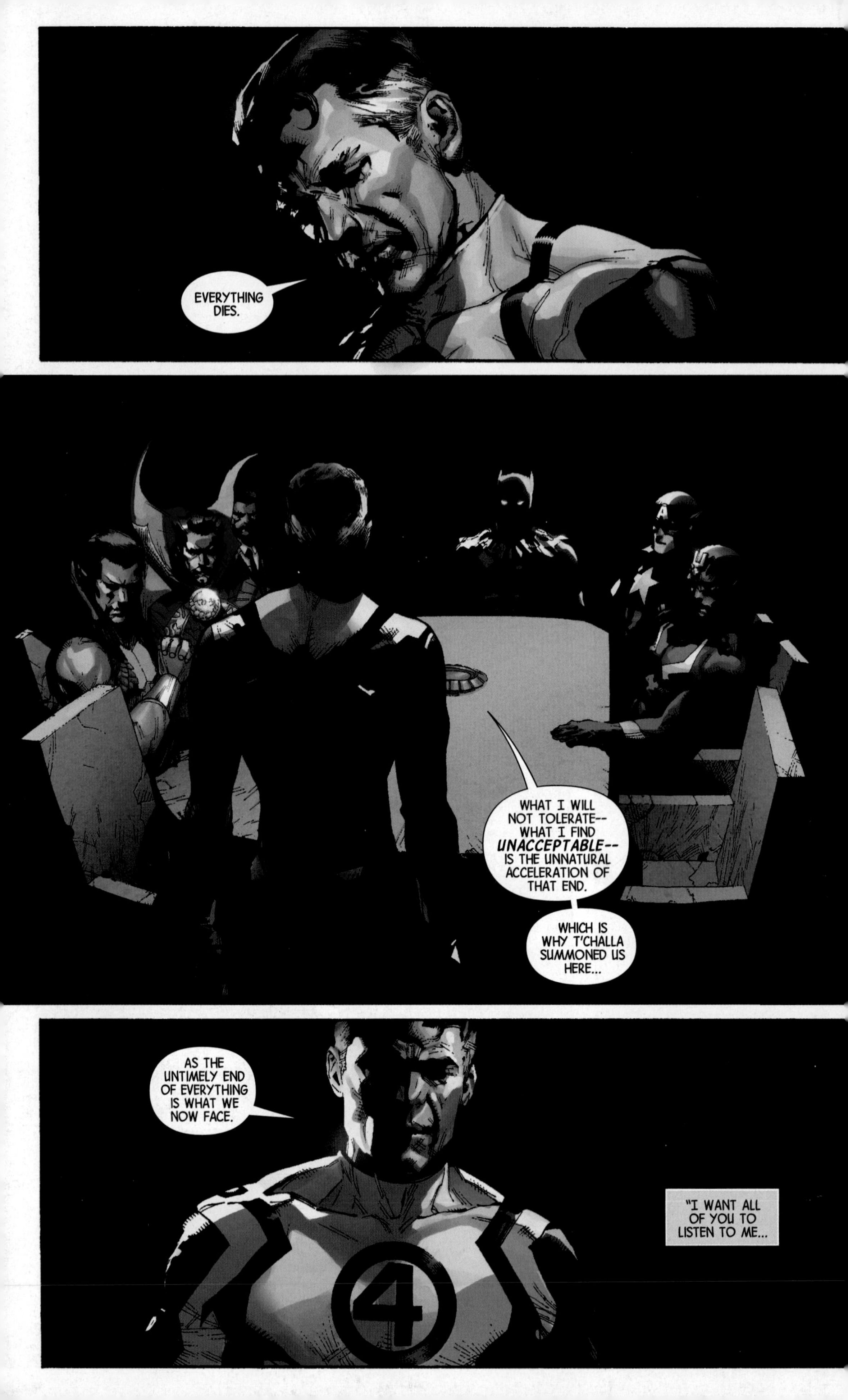
EVERYTHING DIES.
WHAT I WILL NOT TOLERATE-- WHAT I FIND UNACCEPTABLE-- IS THE UNNATURAL ACCELERATION OF THAT END.
WHICH IS WHY T'CHALLA SUMMONED US HERE...
AS THE UNTIMELY END OF EVERYTHING IS WHAT WE NOW FACE.
"I WANT ALL OF YOU TO LISTEN TO ME...

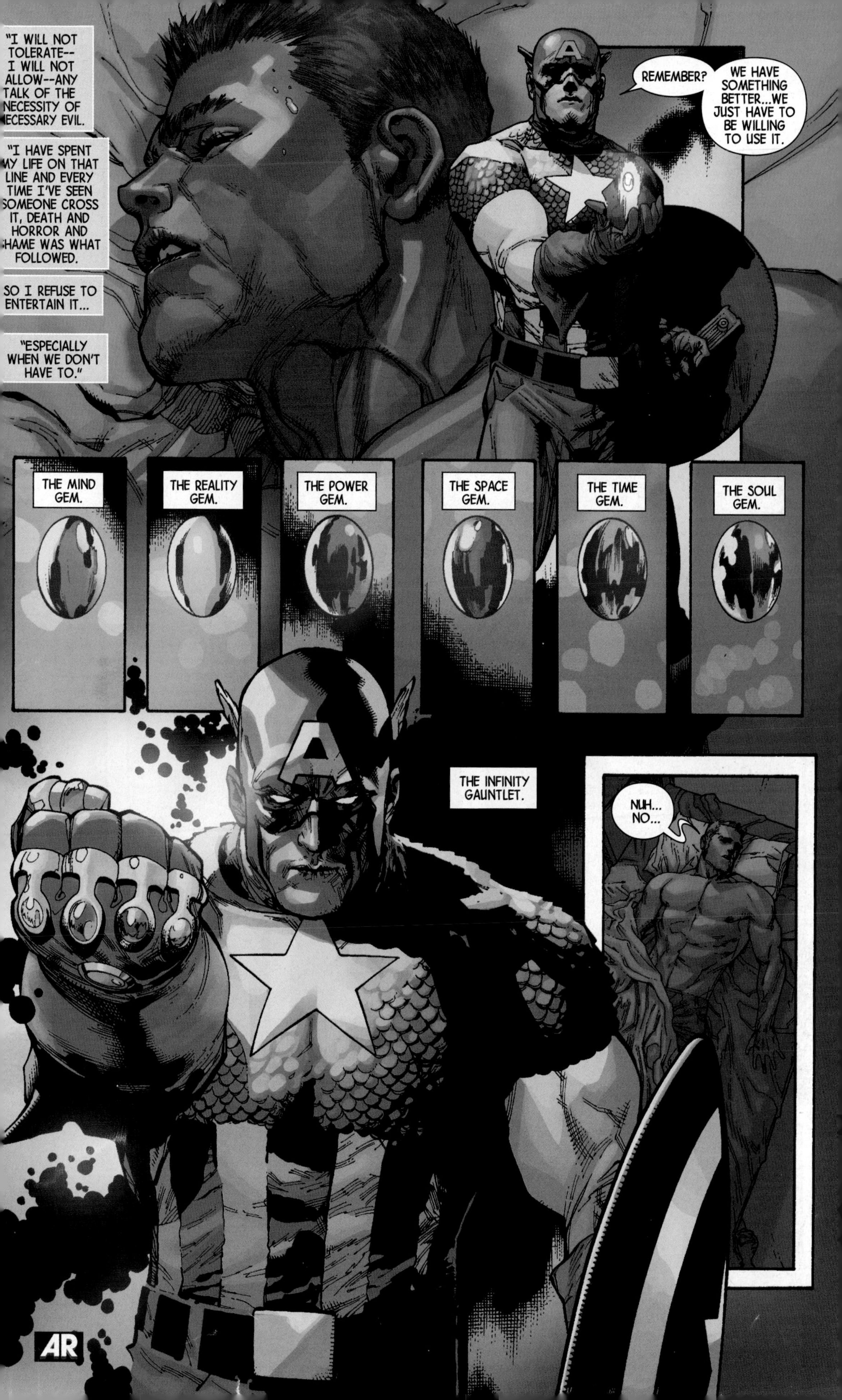

"I WILL NOT TOLERATE-- I WILL NOT ALLOW--ANY TALK OF THE NECESSITY OF NECESSARY EVIL.
"I HAVE SPENT MY LIFE ON THAT LINE AND EVERY TIME I'VE SEEN SOMEONE CROSS IT, DEATH AND HORROR AND SHAME WAS WHAT FOLLOWED.
SO I REFUSE TO ENTERTAIN IT...
"ESPECIALLY WHEN WE DON'T HAVE TO."
REMEMBER?
WE HAVE SOMETHING BETTER...WE JUST HAVE TO BE WILLING TO USE IT.
THE MIND GEM.
THE REALITY GEM.
THE POWER GEM.
THE SPACE GEM.
THE TIME GEM.
THE SOUL GEM.
THE INFINITY GAUNTLET.
NUH... NO...
AR

AHHH!

POWER.

SO MUCH... POWER.

I CAN CONTROL THE HEAVENS...I CAN CONTROL THE EARTH.

STEVE! YOU HAVE TO PUSH IT AWAY! YOU HAVE TO SEND IT BACK TO END THE INCURSION!

IT'S GOING TO WORK. HE'S DONE IT.

YES, BUT... BUT...CAN YOU FEEL THAT?

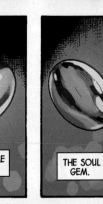

SOMETHING'S NOT RIGHT. SOME VIBRATION. FEEDBACK...

THE MIND GEM.

THE REALITY GEM.

THE POWER GEM.

THE SPACE GEM.

THE TIME GEM.

THE SOUL GEM.

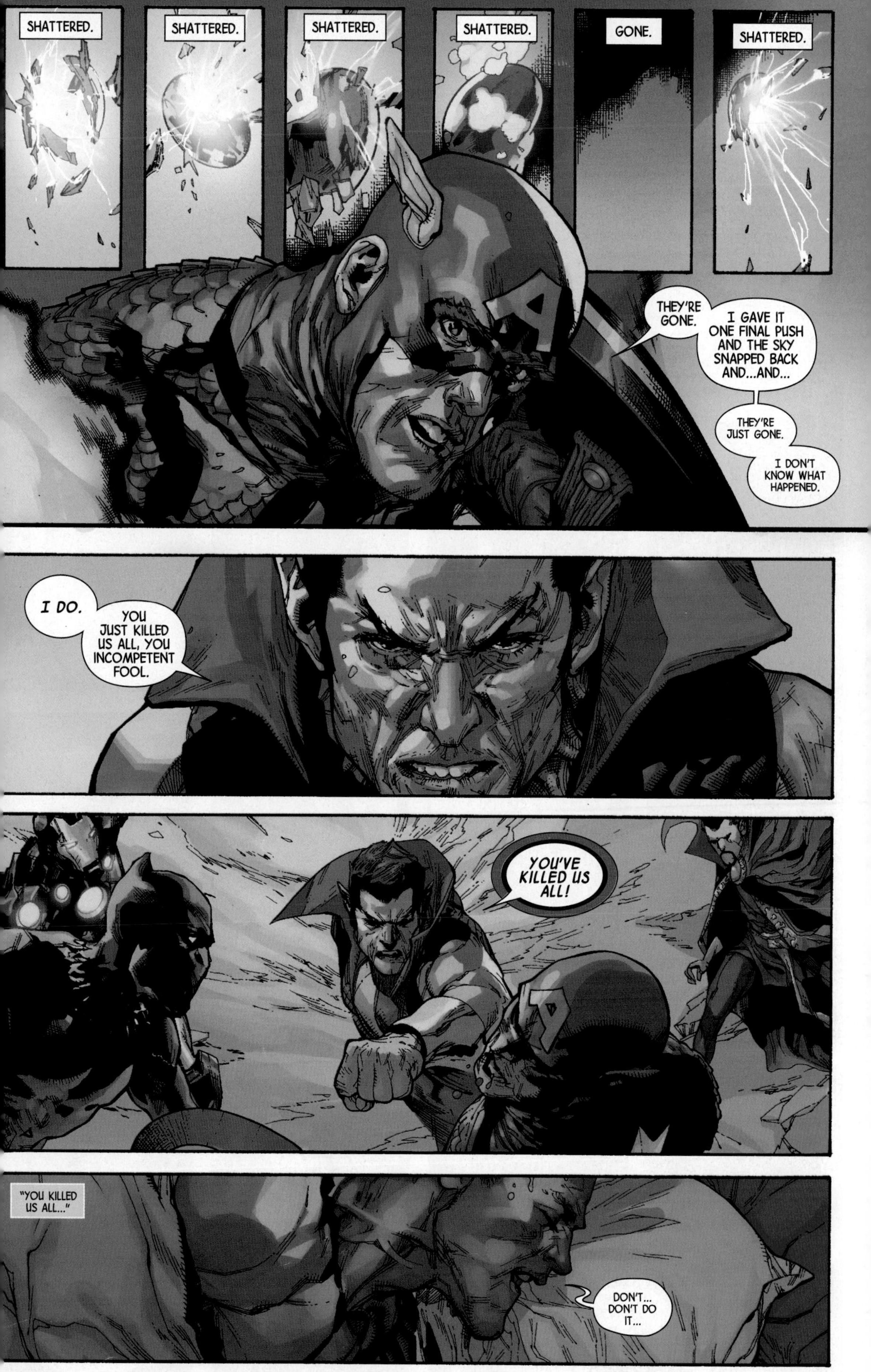
SHATTERED.
SHATTERED.
SHATTERED.
SHATTERED.
GONE.
SHATTERED.
THEY'RE GONE.
I GAVE IT ONE FINAL PUSH AND THE SKY SNAPPED BACK AND...AND...
THEY'RE JUST GONE.
I DON'T KNOW WHAT HAPPENED.
I DO.
YOU JUST KILLED US ALL, YOU INCOMPETENT FOOL.
YOU'VE KILLED US ALL!
"YOU KILLED US ALL..."
DON'T... DON'T DO IT...

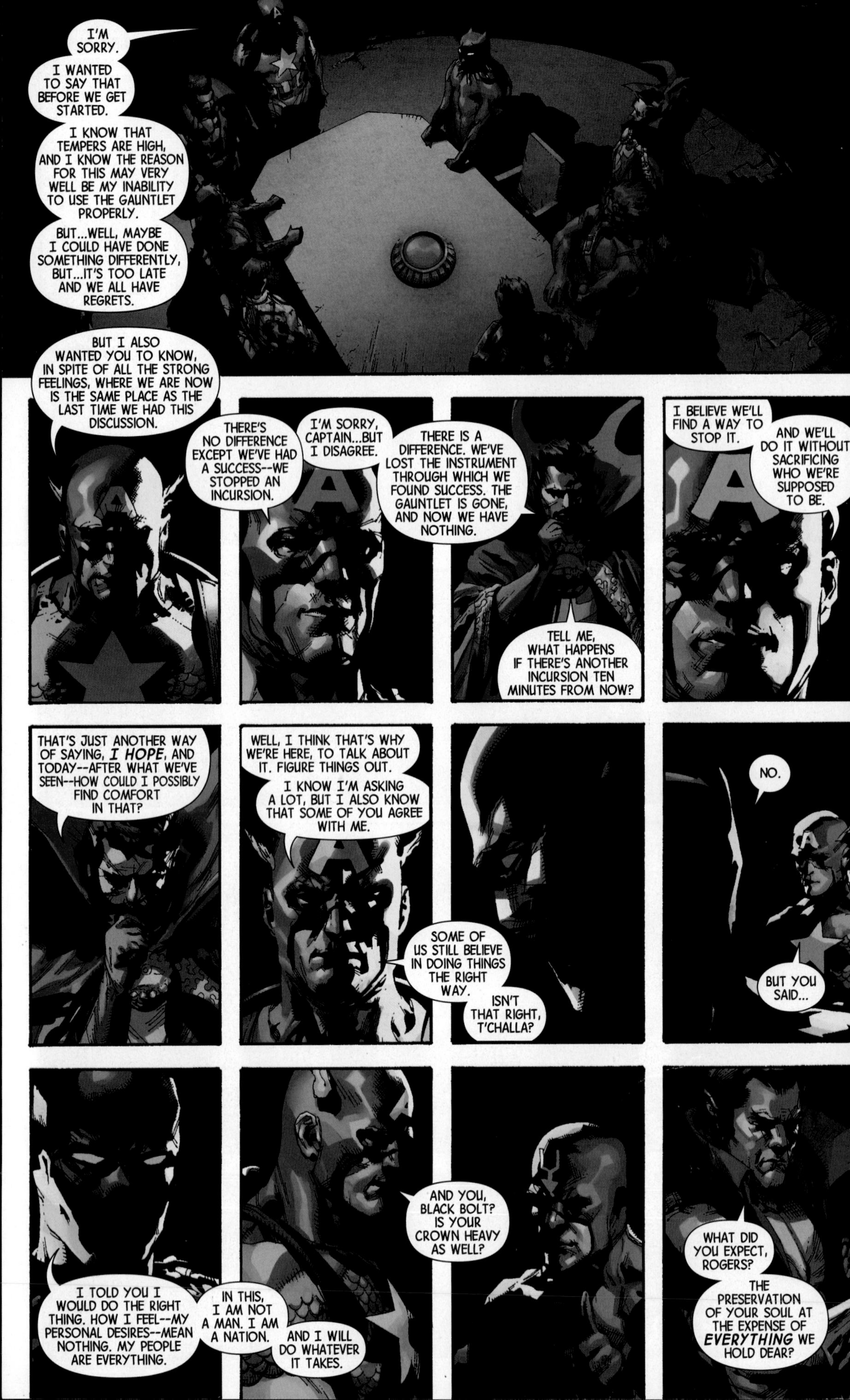
I'M SORRY.
I WANTED TO SAY THAT BEFORE WE GET STARTED.
I KNOW THAT TEMPERS ARE HIGH, AND I KNOW THE REASON FOR THIS MAY VERY WELL BE MY INABILITY TO USE THE GAUNTLET PROPERLY.
BUT...WELL, MAYBE I COULD HAVE DONE SOMETHING DIFFERENTLY, BUT...IT'S TOO LATE AND WE ALL HAVE REGRETS.
BUT I ALSO WANTED YOU TO KNOW, IN SPITE OF ALL THE STRONG FEELINGS, WHERE WE ARE NOW IS THE SAME PLACE AS THE LAST TIME WE HAD THIS DISCUSSION.
THERE'S NO DIFFERENCE EXCEPT WE'VE HAD A SUCCESS--WE STOPPED AN INCURSION.
I'M SORRY, CAPTAIN...BUT I DISAGREE.
THERE IS A DIFFERENCE. WE'VE LOST THE INSTRUMENT THROUGH WHICH WE FOUND SUCCESS. THE GAUNTLET IS GONE, AND NOW WE HAVE NOTHING.
TELL ME, WHAT HAPPENS IF THERE'S ANOTHER INCURSION TEN MINUTES FROM NOW?
I BELIEVE WE'LL FIND A WAY TO STOP IT.
AND WE'LL DO IT WITHOUT SACRIFICING WHO WE'RE SUPPOSED TO BE.
THAT'S JUST ANOTHER WAY OF SAYING, *I HOPE*, AND TODAY--AFTER WHAT WE'VE SEEN--HOW COULD I POSSIBLY FIND COMFORT IN THAT?
WELL, I THINK THAT'S WHY WE'RE HERE, TO TALK ABOUT IT. FIGURE THINGS OUT.
I KNOW I'M ASKING A LOT, BUT I ALSO KNOW THAT SOME OF YOU AGREE WITH ME.
SOME OF US STILL BELIEVE IN DOING THINGS THE RIGHT WAY.
ISN'T THAT RIGHT, T'CHALLA?
NO.
BUT YOU SAID...
I TOLD YOU I WOULD DO THE RIGHT THING. HOW I FEEL--MY PERSONAL DESIRES--MEAN NOTHING. MY PEOPLE ARE EVERYTHING.
IN THIS, I AM NOT A MAN. I AM A NATION.
AND I WILL DO WHATEVER IT TAKES.
AND YOU, BLACK BOLT? IS YOUR CROWN HEAVY AS WELL?
WHAT DID YOU EXPECT, ROGERS?
THE PRESERVATION OF YOUR SOUL AT THE EXPENSE OF *EVERYTHING* WE HOLD DEAR?

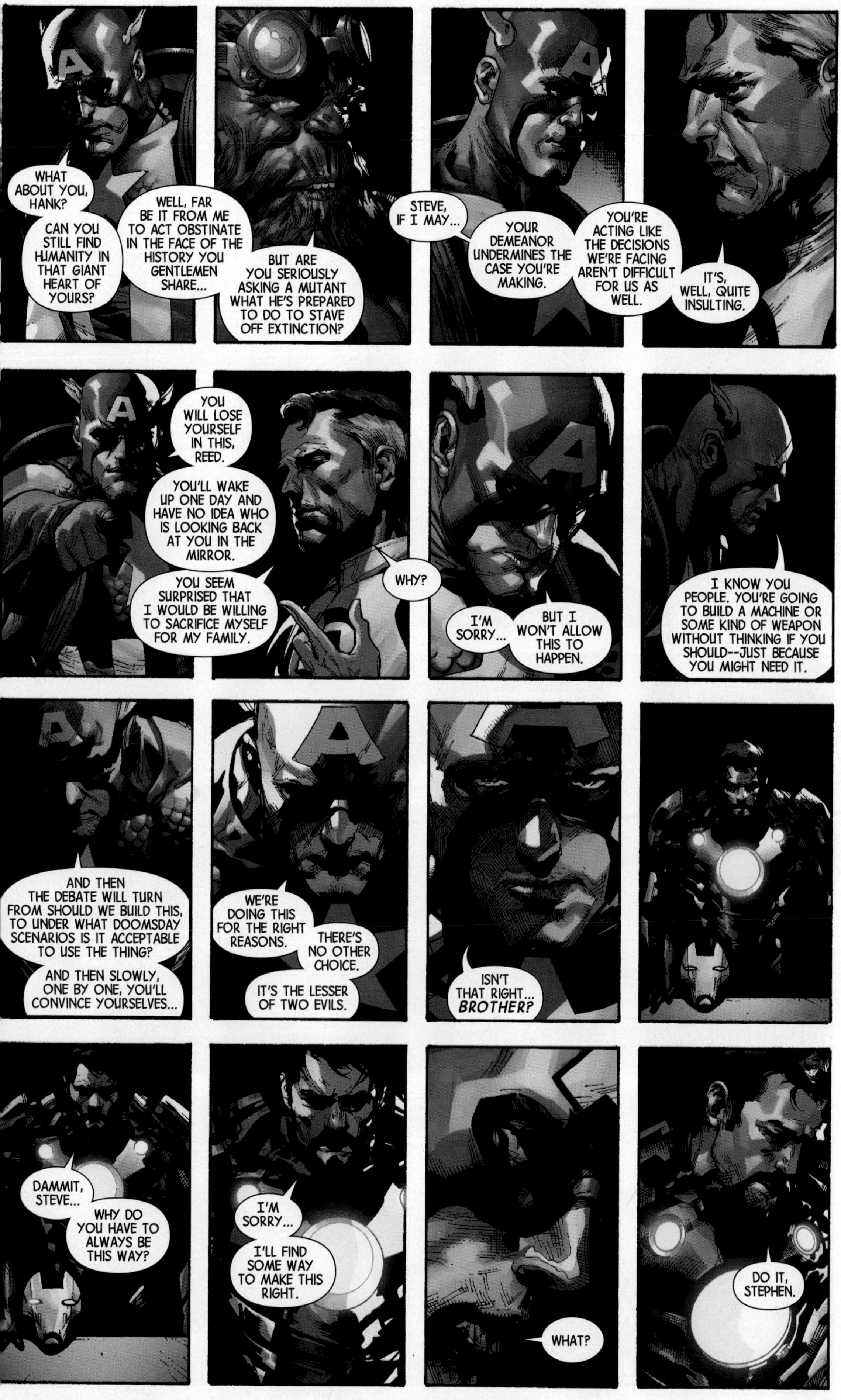
WHAT ABOUT YOU, HANK?
CAN YOU STILL FIND HUMANITY IN THAT GIANT HEART OF YOURS?
WELL, FAR BE IT FROM ME TO ACT OBSTINATE IN THE FACE OF THE HISTORY YOU GENTLEMEN SHARE...
BUT ARE YOU SERIOUSLY ASKING A MUTANT WHAT HE'S PREPARED TO DO TO STAVE OFF EXTINCTION?
STEVE, IF I MAY...
YOUR DEMEANOR UNDERMINES THE CASE YOU'RE MAKING.
YOU'RE ACTING LIKE THE DECISIONS WE'RE FACING AREN'T DIFFICULT FOR US AS WELL.
IT'S, WELL, QUITE INSULTING.
YOU WILL LOSE YOURSELF IN THIS, REED.
YOU'LL WAKE UP ONE DAY AND HAVE NO IDEA WHO IS LOOKING BACK AT YOU IN THE MIRROR.
YOU SEEM SURPRISED THAT I WOULD BE WILLING TO SACRIFICE MYSELF FOR MY FAMILY.
WHY?
I'M SORRY...
BUT I WON'T ALLOW THIS TO HAPPEN.
I KNOW YOU PEOPLE. YOU'RE GOING TO BUILD A MACHINE OR SOME KIND OF WEAPON WITHOUT THINKING IF YOU SHOULD--JUST BECAUSE YOU MIGHT NEED IT.
AND THEN THE DEBATE WILL TURN FROM SHOULD WE BUILD THIS, TO UNDER WHAT DOOMSDAY SCENARIOS IS IT ACCEPTABLE TO USE THE THING?
AND THEN SLOWLY, ONE BY ONE, YOU'LL CONVINCE YOURSELVES...
WE'RE DOING THIS FOR THE RIGHT REASONS.
THERE'S NO OTHER CHOICE.
IT'S THE LESSER OF TWO EVILS.
ISN'T THAT RIGHT... *BROTHER?*
DAMMIT, STEVE...
WHY DO YOU HAVE TO ALWAYS BE THIS WAY?
I'M SORRY...
I'LL FIND SOME WAY TO MAKE THIS RIGHT.
WHAT?
DO IT, STEPHEN.

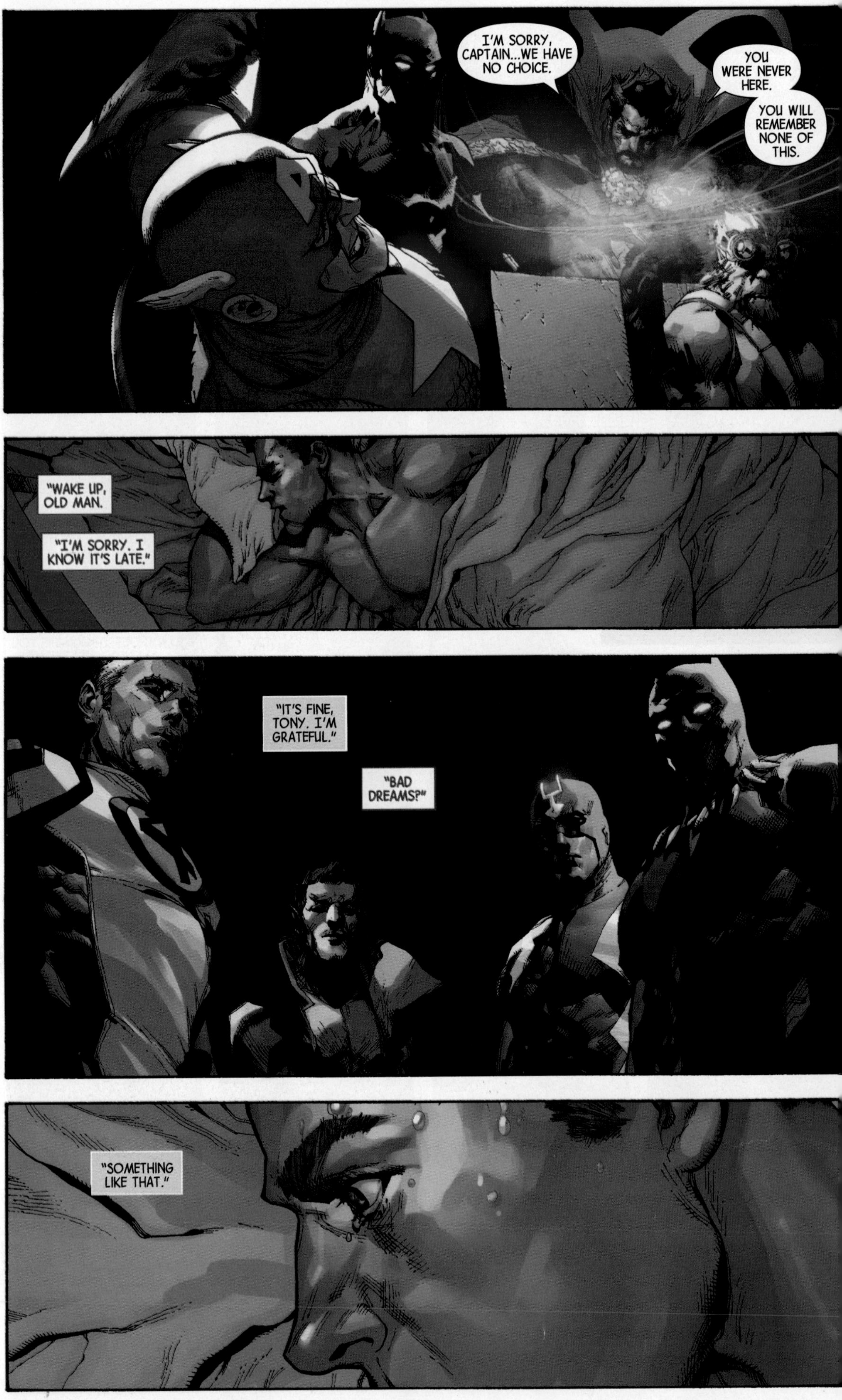
I'M SORRY, CAPTAIN...WE HAVE NO CHOICE.
YOU WERE NEVER HERE.
YOU WILL REMEMBER NONE OF THIS.
"WAKE UP, OLD MAN.
"I'M SORRY. I KNOW IT'S LATE."
"IT'S FINE, TONY. I'M GRATEFUL."
"BAD DREAMS?"
"SOMETHING LIKE THAT."

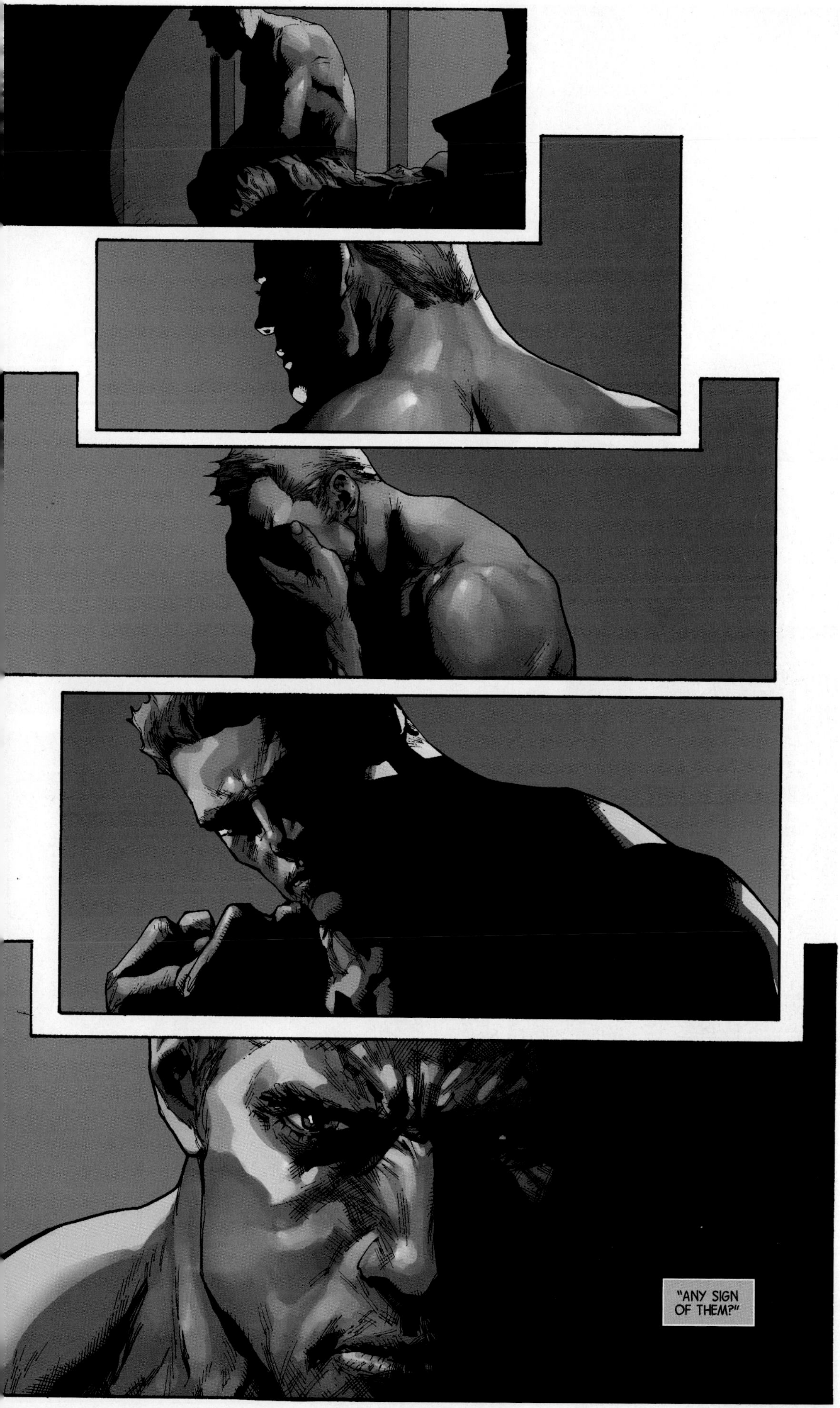
"ANY SIGN OF THEM?"

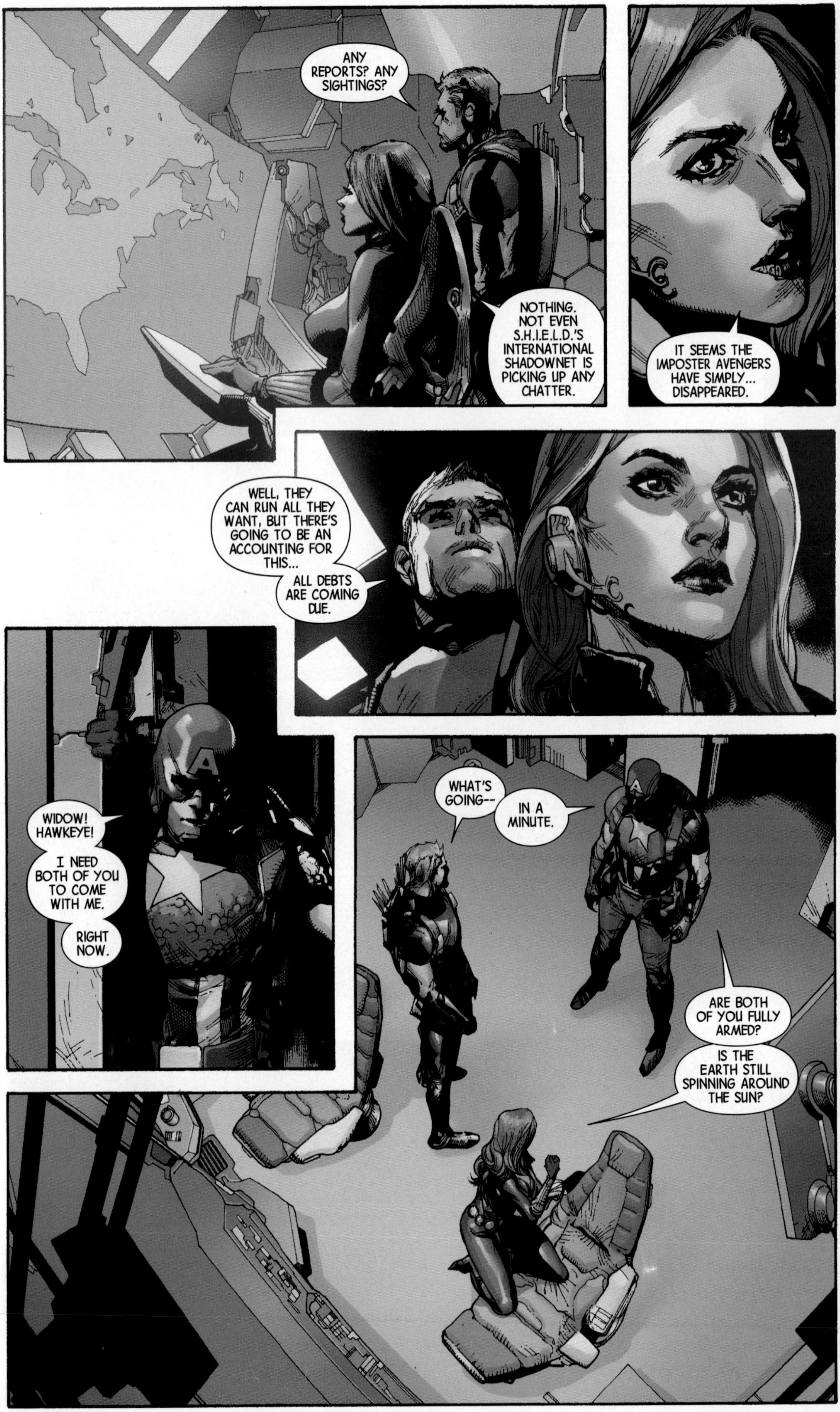
ANY REPORTS? ANY SIGHTINGS?
NOTHING. NOT EVEN S.H.I.E.L.D.'S INTERNATIONAL SHADOWNET IS PICKING UP ANY CHATTER.
IT SEEMS THE IMPOSTER AVENGERS HAVE SIMPLY... DISAPPEARED.
WELL, THEY CAN RUN ALL THEY WANT, BUT THERE'S GOING TO BE AN ACCOUNTING FOR THIS...
ALL DEBTS ARE COMING DUE.
WIDOW! HAWKEYE!
I NEED BOTH OF YOU TO COME WITH ME.
RIGHT NOW.
WHAT'S GOING--
IN A MINUTE.
ARE BOTH OF YOU FULLY ARMED?
IS THE EARTH STILL SPINNING AROUND THE SUN?

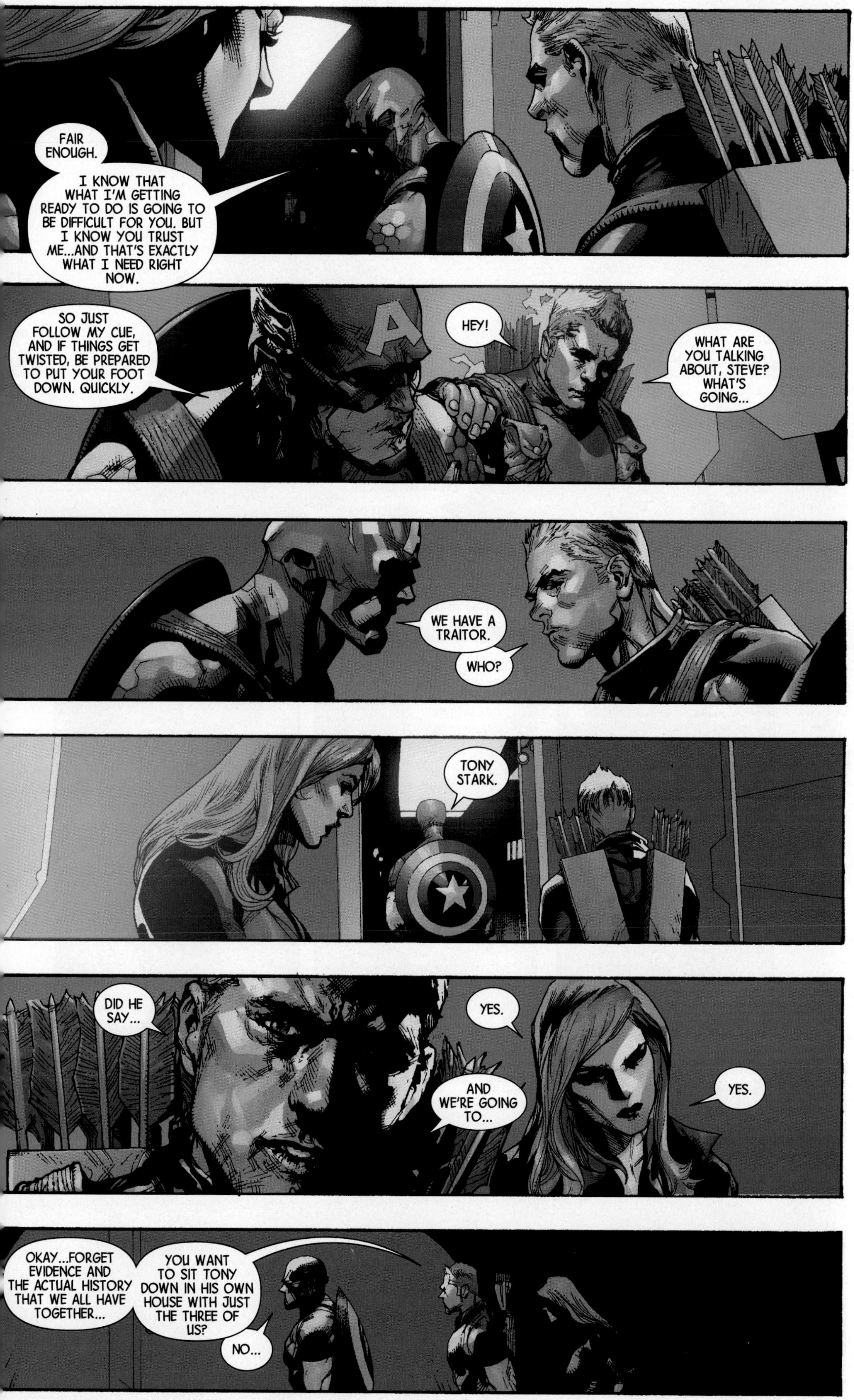
FAIR ENOUGH.
I KNOW THAT WHAT I'M GETTING READY TO DO IS GOING TO BE DIFFICULT FOR YOU. BUT I KNOW YOU TRUST ME...AND THAT'S EXACTLY WHAT I NEED RIGHT NOW.
SO JUST FOLLOW MY CUE, AND IF THINGS GET TWISTED, BE PREPARED TO PUT YOUR FOOT DOWN. QUICKLY.
HEY!
WHAT ARE YOU TALKING ABOUT, STEVE? WHAT'S GOING...
WE HAVE A TRAITOR.
WHO?
TONY STARK.
DID HE SAY...
YES.
AND WE'RE GOING TO...
YES.
OKAY...FORGET EVIDENCE AND THE ACTUAL HISTORY THAT WE ALL HAVE TOGETHER...
YOU WANT TO SIT TONY DOWN IN HIS OWN HOUSE WITH JUST THE THREE OF US?
NO...

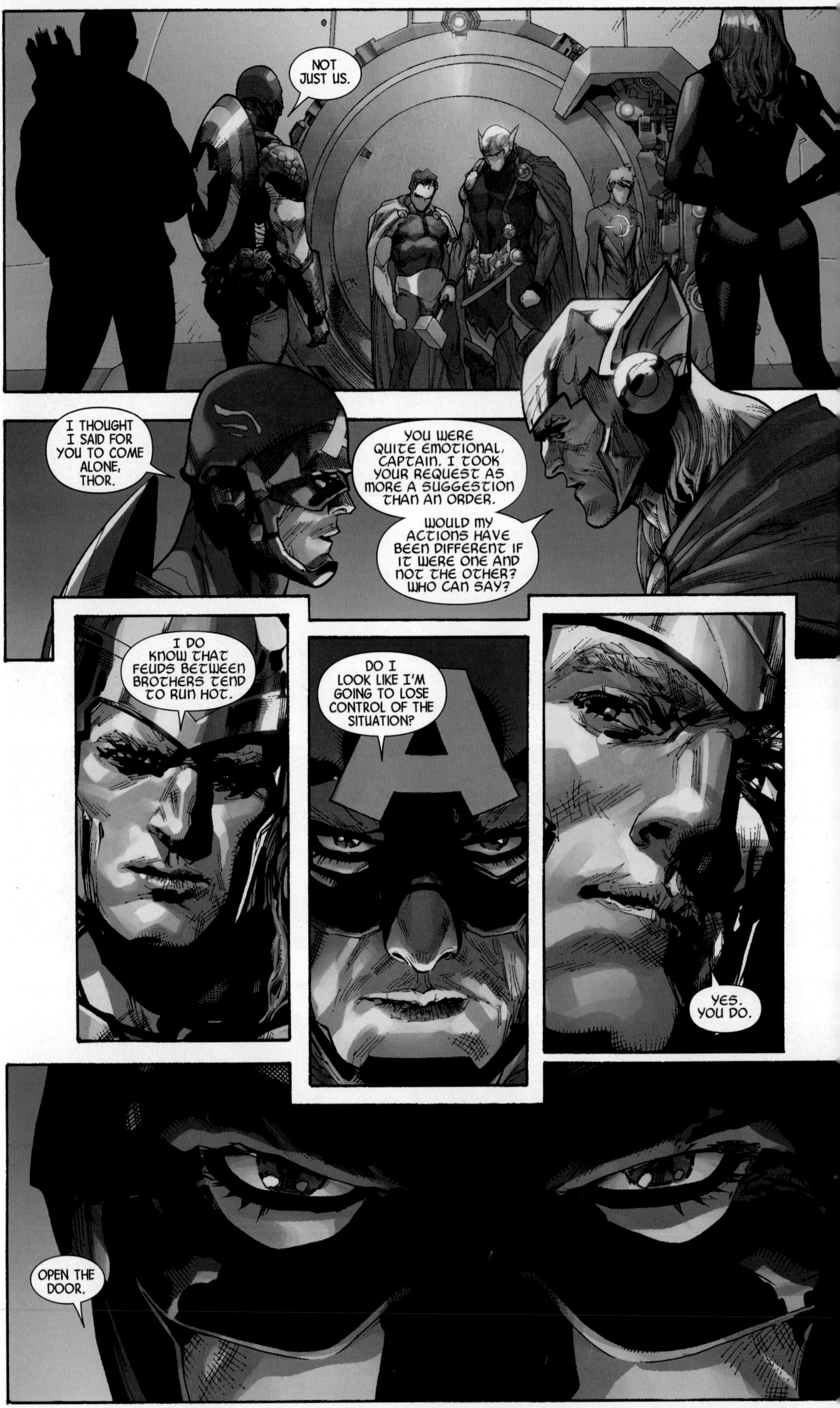
NOT JUST US.
I THOUGHT I SAID FOR YOU TO COME ALONE, THOR.
YOU WERE QUITE EMOTIONAL, CAPTAIN. I TOOK YOUR REQUEST AS MORE A SUGGESTION THAN AN ORDER.
WOULD MY ACTIONS HAVE BEEN DIFFERENT IF IT WERE ONE AND NOT THE OTHER? WHO CAN SAY?
I DO KNOW THAT FEUDS BETWEEN BROTHERS TEND TO RUN HOT.
DO I LOOK LIKE I'M GOING TO LOSE CONTROL OF THE SITUATION?
YES. YOU DO.
OPEN THE DOOR.

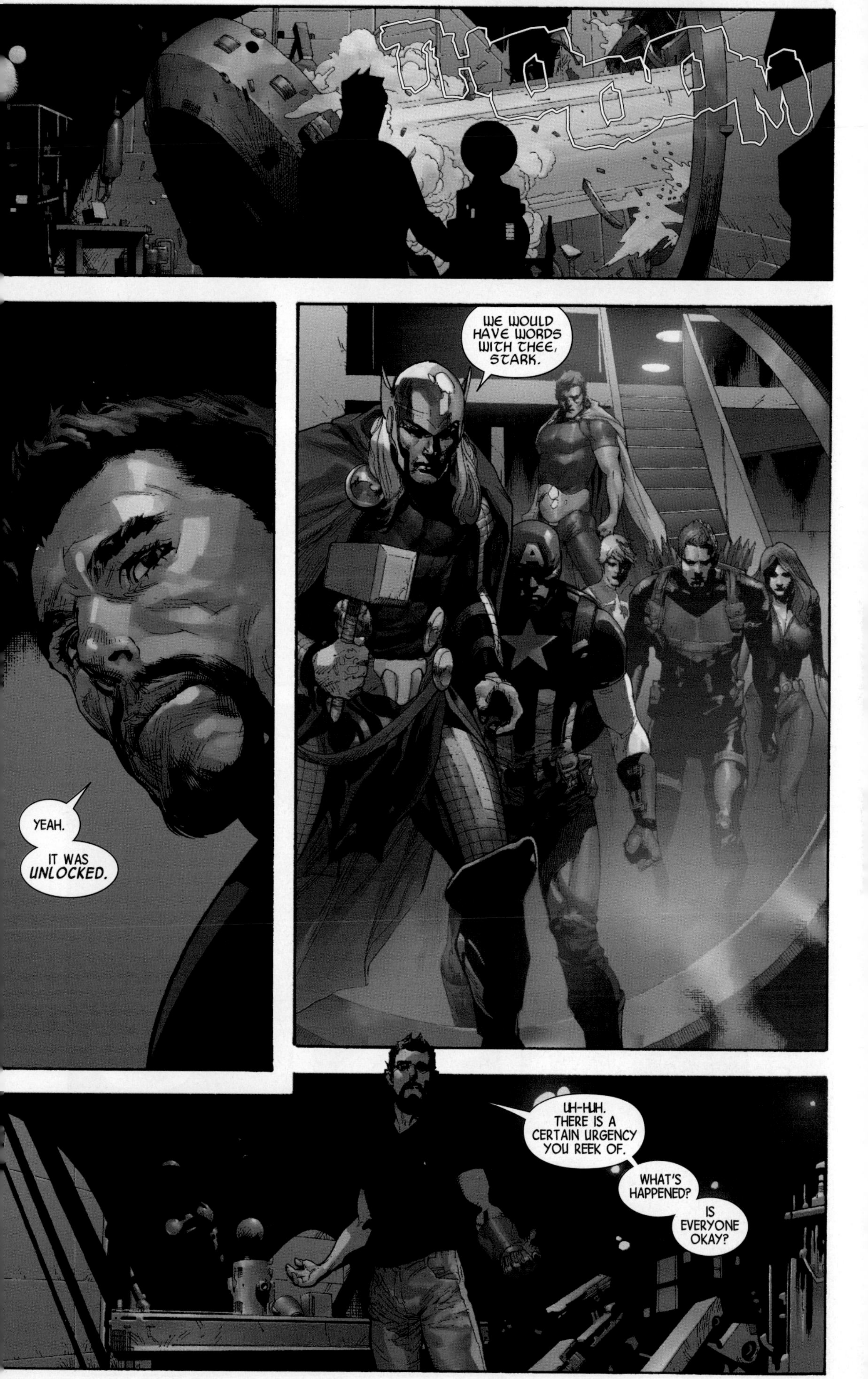
THOOOOM
YEAH.
IT WAS UNLOCKED.
WE WOULD HAVE WORDS WITH THEE, STARK.
UH-HUH. THERE IS A CERTAIN URGENCY YOU REEK OF.
WHAT'S HAPPENED?
IS EVERYONE OKAY?

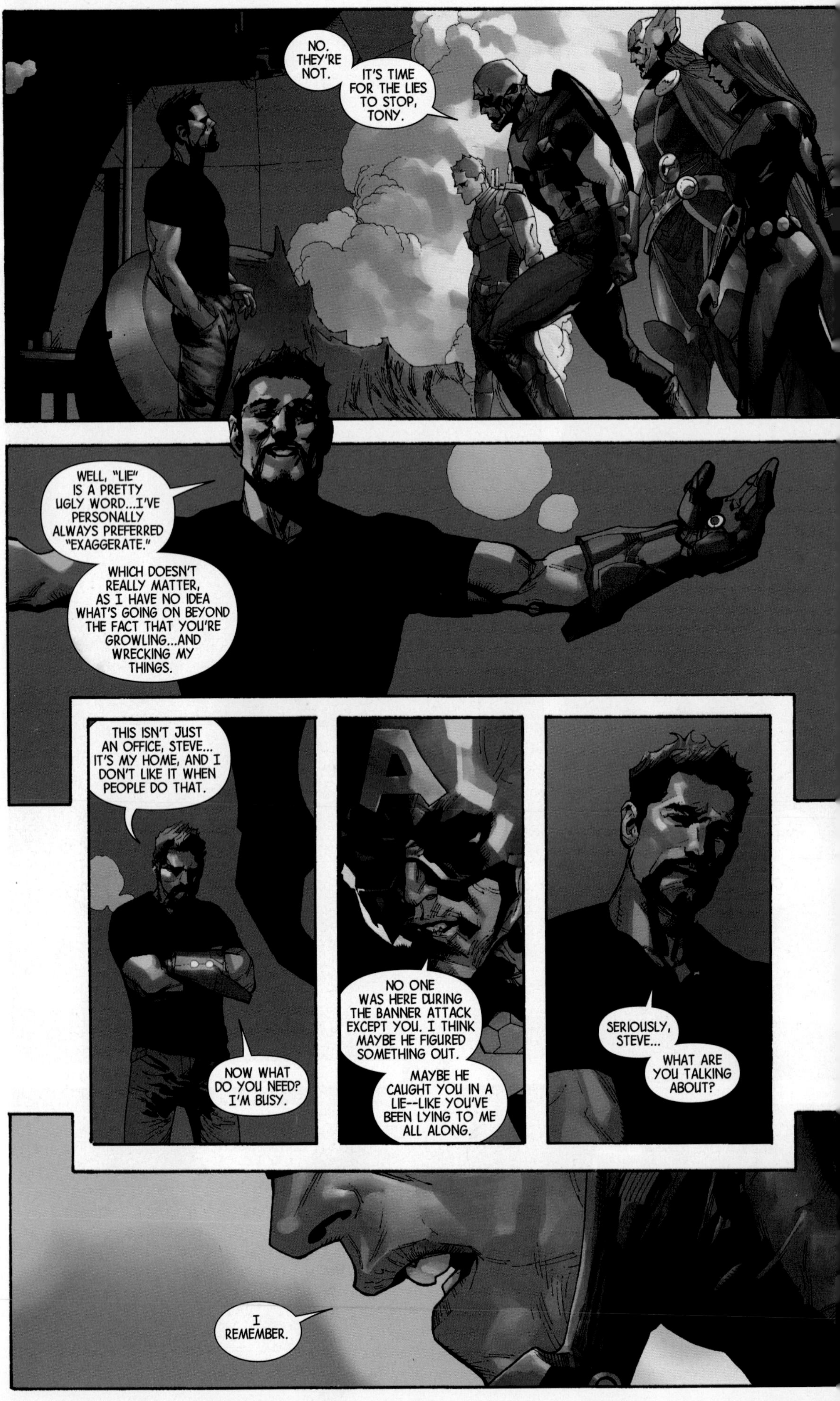
NO. THEY'RE NOT.
IT'S TIME FOR THE LIES TO STOP, TONY.
WELL, "LIE" IS A PRETTY UGLY WORD...I'VE PERSONALLY ALWAYS PREFERRED "EXAGGERATE."
WHICH DOESN'T REALLY MATTER, AS I HAVE NO IDEA WHAT'S GOING ON BEYOND THE FACT THAT YOU'RE GROWLING...AND WRECKING MY THINGS.
THIS ISN'T JUST AN OFFICE, STEVE... IT'S MY HOME, AND I DON'T LIKE IT WHEN PEOPLE DO THAT.
NOW WHAT DO YOU NEED? I'M BUSY.
NO ONE WAS HERE DURING THE BANNER ATTACK EXCEPT YOU. I THINK MAYBE HE FIGURED SOMETHING OUT.
MAYBE HE CAUGHT YOU IN A LIE--LIKE YOU'VE BEEN LYING TO ME ALL ALONG.
SERIOUSLY, STEVE...
WHAT ARE YOU TALKING ABOUT?
I REMEMBER.

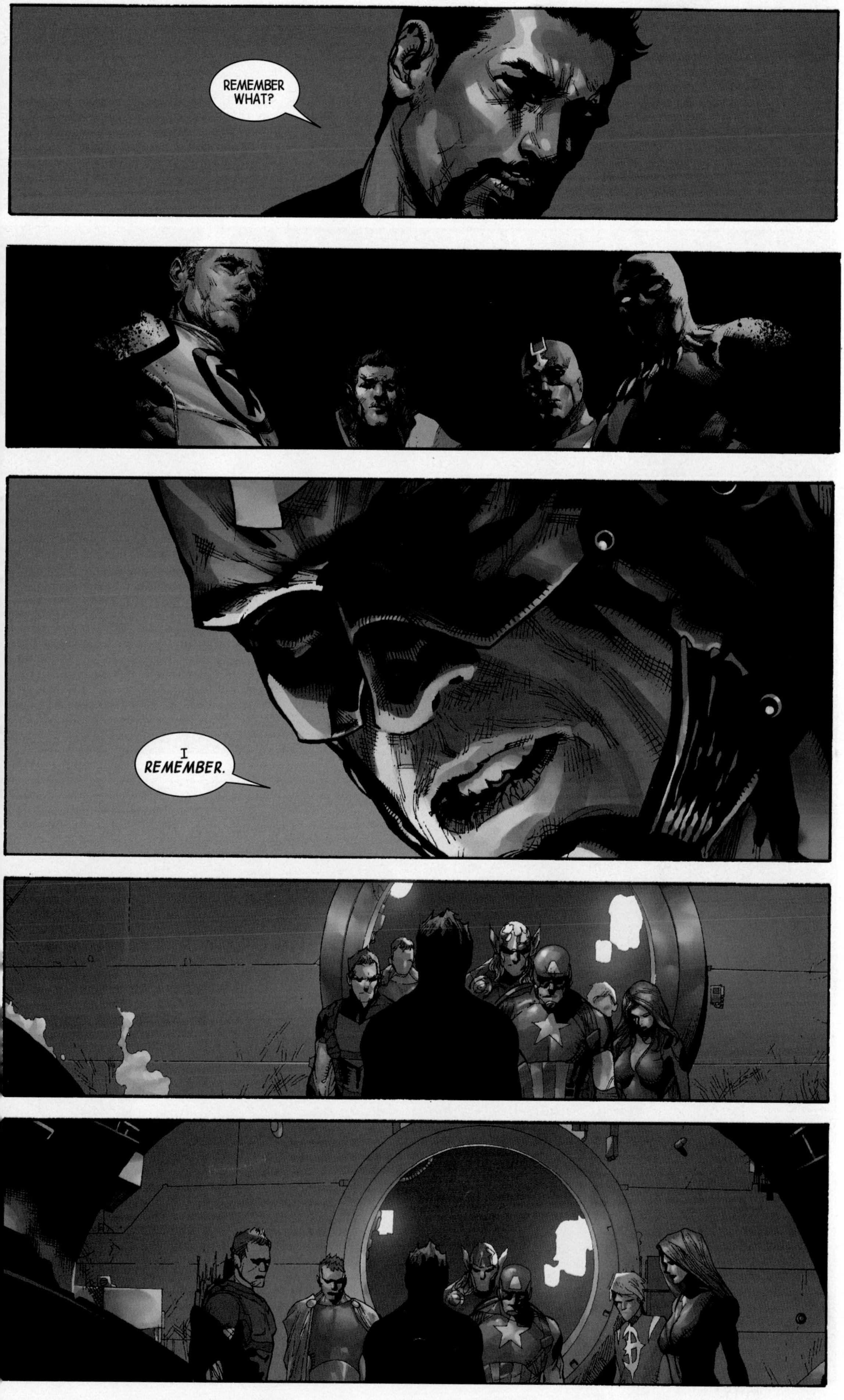
REMEMBER WHAT?
I REMEMBER.

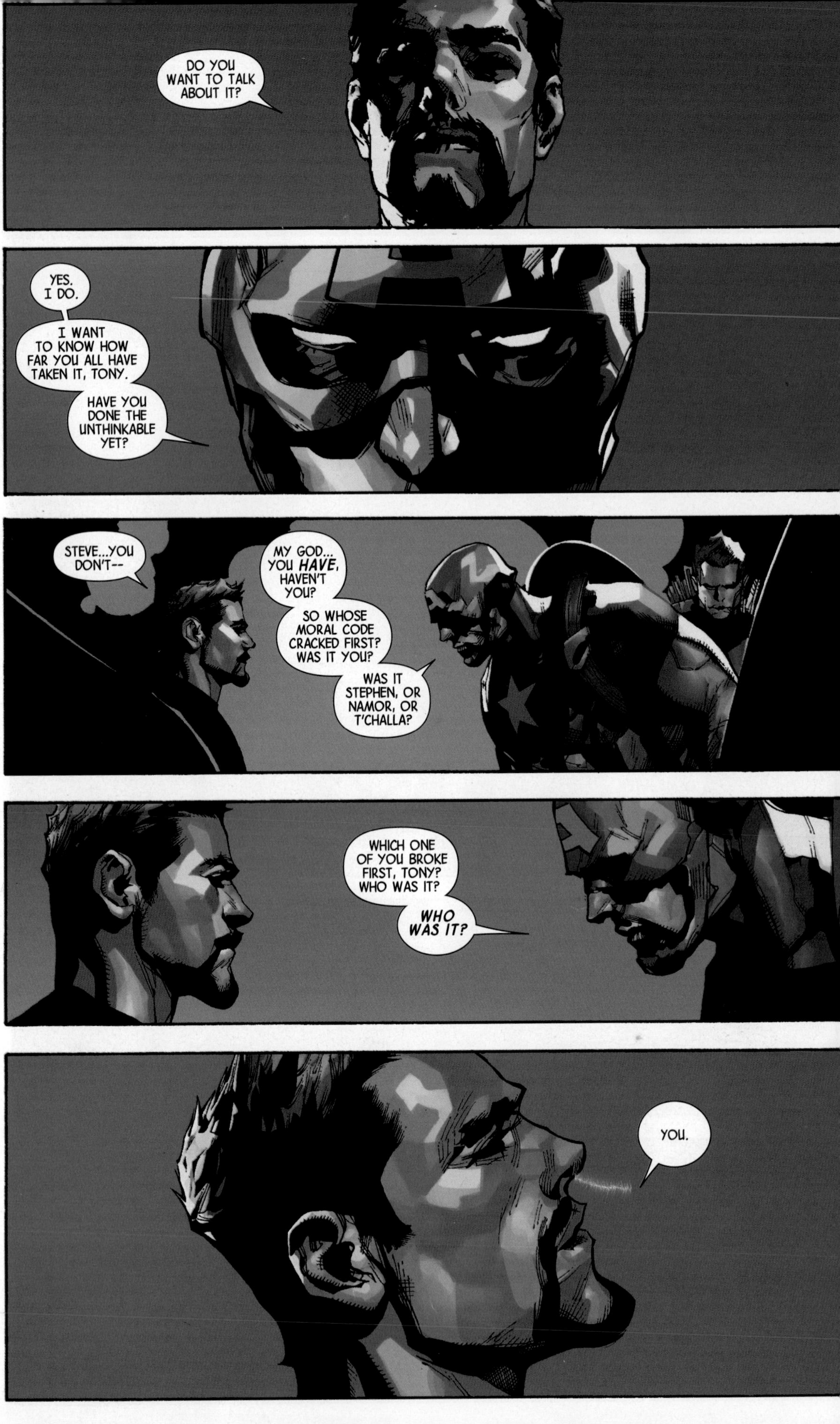
DO YOU WANT TO TALK ABOUT IT?
YES. I DO.
I WANT TO KNOW HOW FAR YOU ALL HAVE TAKEN IT, TONY.
HAVE YOU DONE THE UNTHINKABLE YET?
STEVE...YOU DON'T--
MY GOD... YOU *HAVE*, HAVEN'T YOU?
SO WHOSE MORAL CODE CRACKED FIRST? WAS IT YOU?
WAS IT STEPHEN, OR NAMOR, OR T'CHALLA?
WHICH ONE OF YOU BROKE FIRST, TONY? WHO WAS IT?
WHO WAS IT?
YOU.

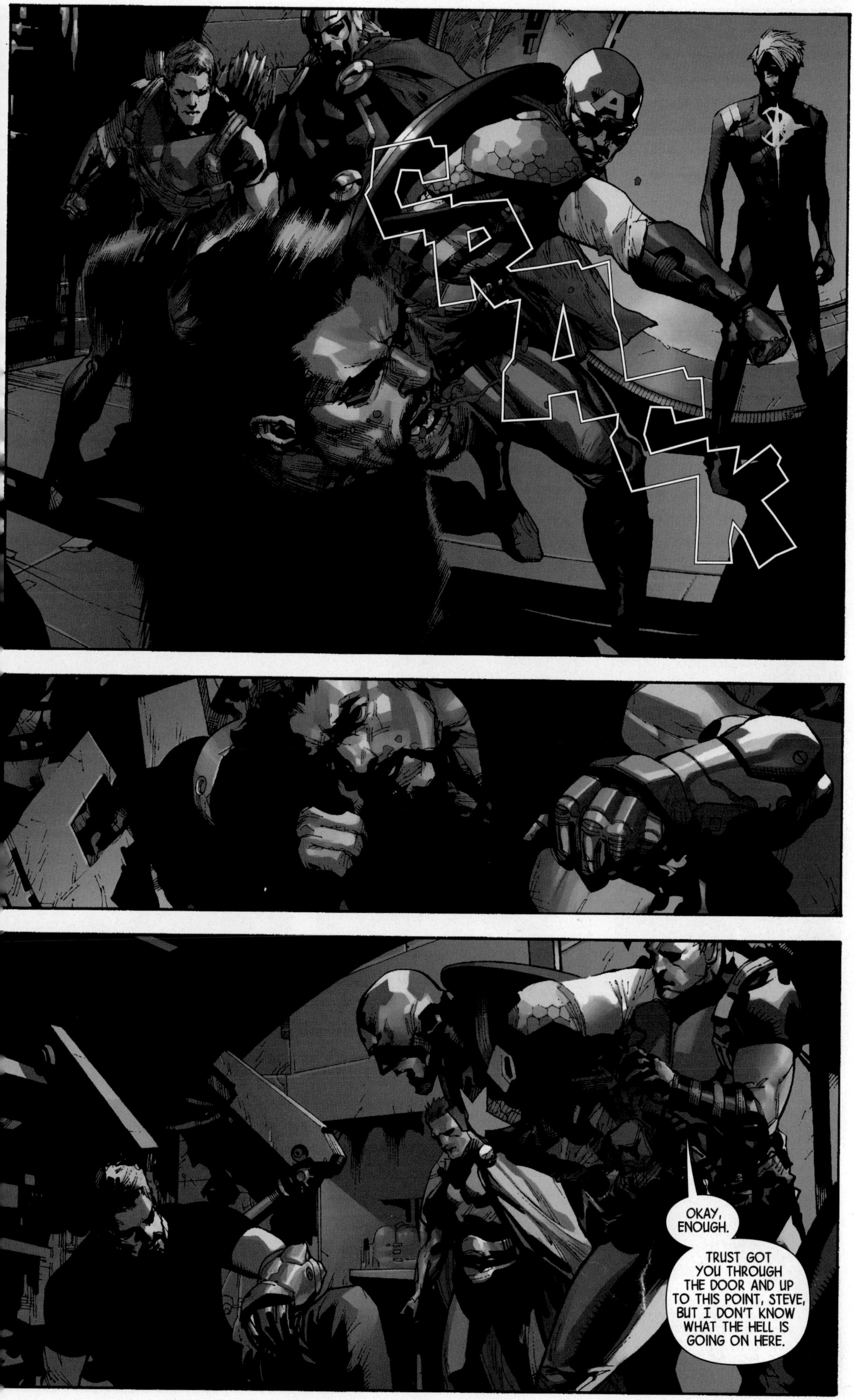
CRACK
OKAY, ENOUGH.
TRUST GOT YOU THROUGH THE DOOR AND UP TO THIS POINT, STEVE, BUT I DON'T KNOW WHAT THE HELL IS GOING ON HERE.

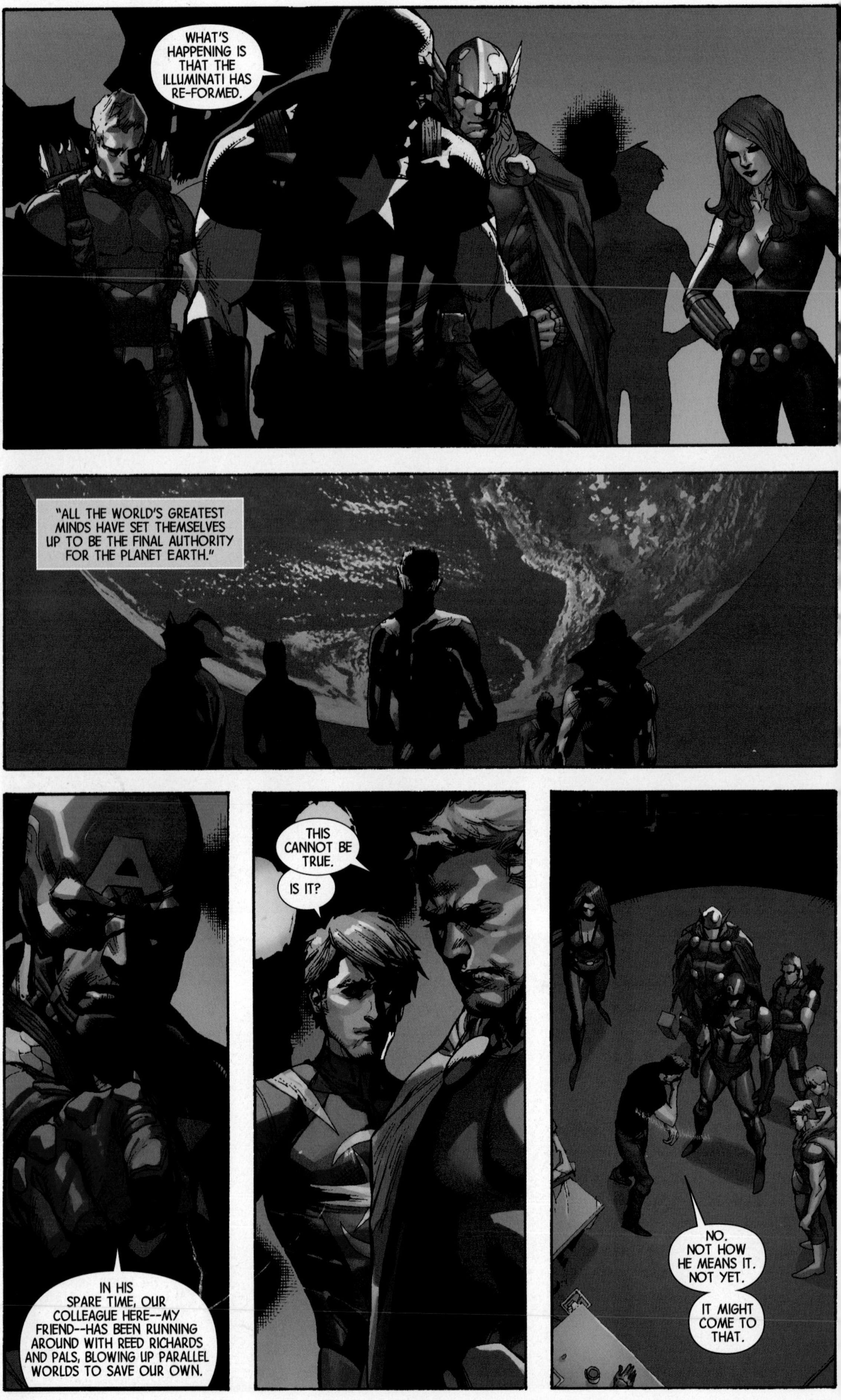
WHAT'S HAPPENING IS THAT THE ILLUMINATI HAS RE-FORMED.
"ALL THE WORLD'S GREATEST MINDS HAVE SET THEMSELVES UP TO BE THE FINAL AUTHORITY FOR THE PLANET EARTH."
IN HIS SPARE TIME, OUR COLLEAGUE HERE--MY FRIEND--HAS BEEN RUNNING AROUND WITH REED RICHARDS AND PALS, BLOWING UP PARALLEL WORLDS TO SAVE OUR OWN.
THIS CANNOT BE TRUE.
IS IT?
NO. NOT HOW HE MEANS IT. NOT YET.
IT MIGHT COME TO THAT.

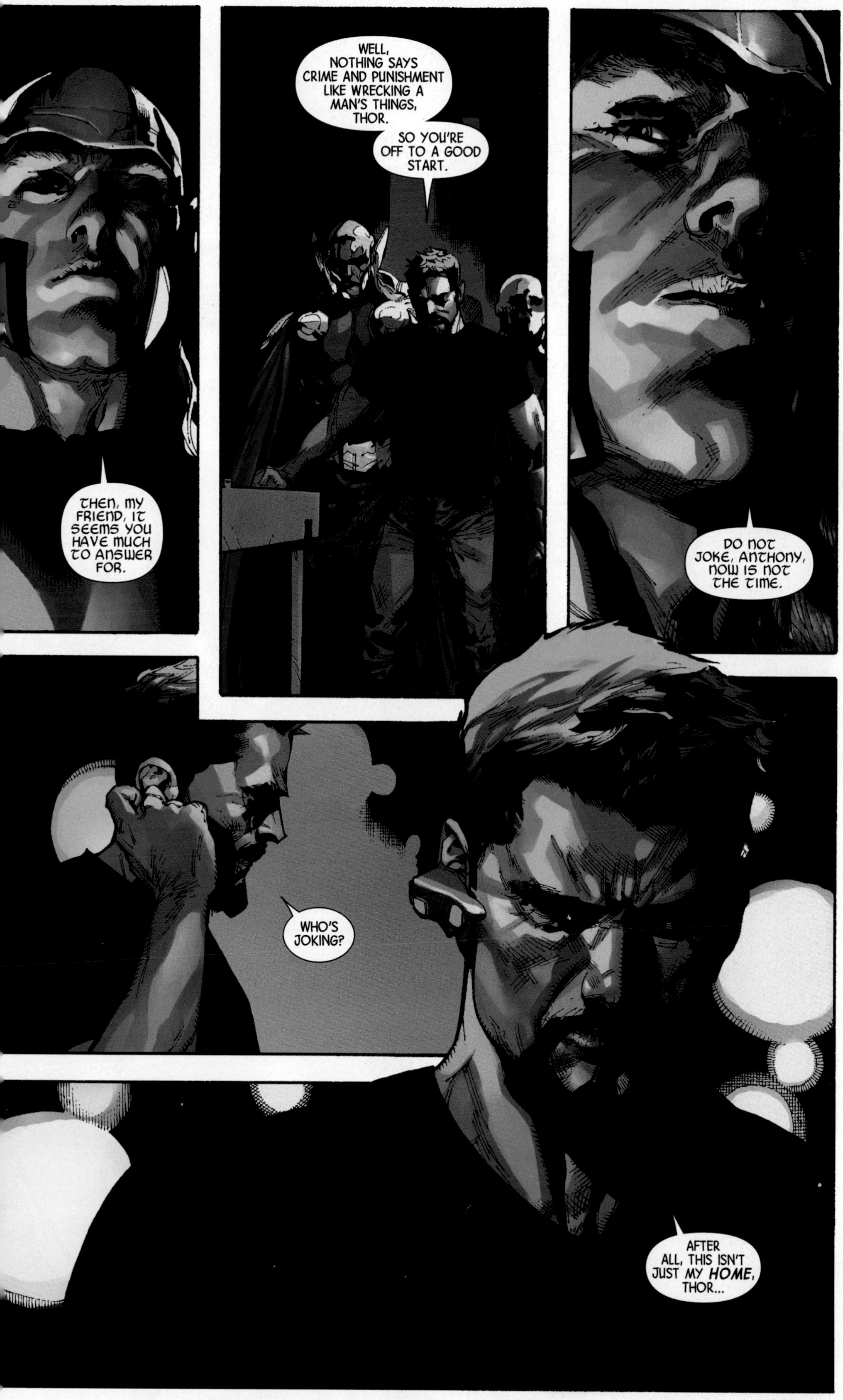
THEN, MY FRIEND, IT SEEMS YOU HAVE MUCH TO ANSWER FOR.
WELL, NOTHING SAYS CRIME AND PUNISHMENT LIKE WRECKING A MAN'S THINGS, THOR.
SO YOU'RE OFF TO A GOOD START.
DO NOT JOKE, ANTHONY, NOW IS NOT THE TIME.
WHO'S JOKING?
AFTER ALL, THIS ISN'T JUST MY HOME, THOR...

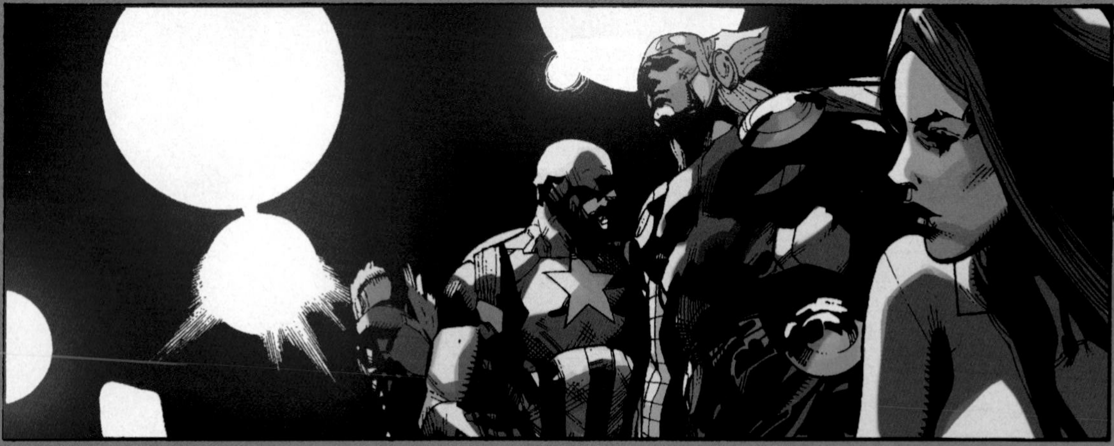

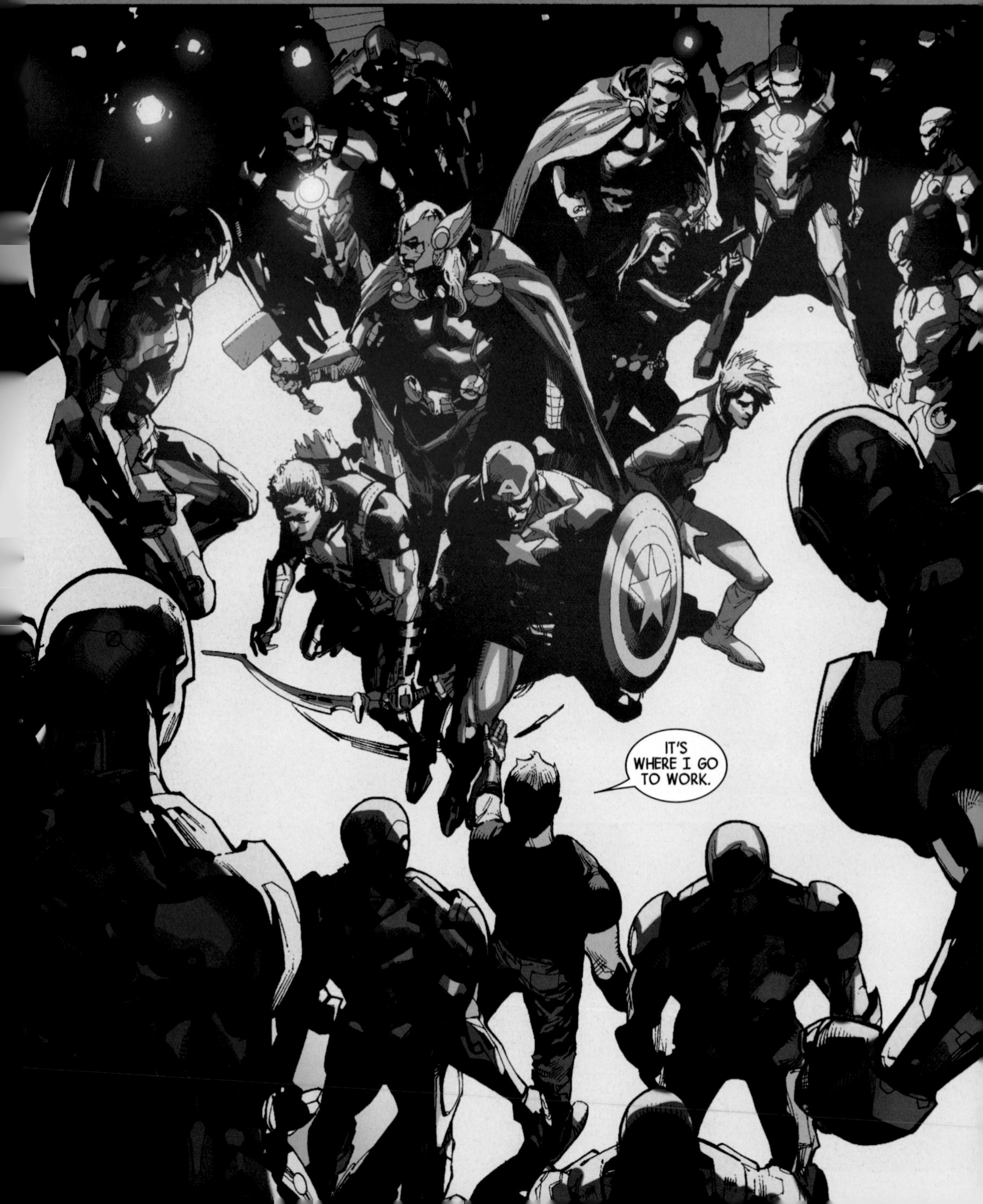
IT'S WHERE I GO TO WORK.

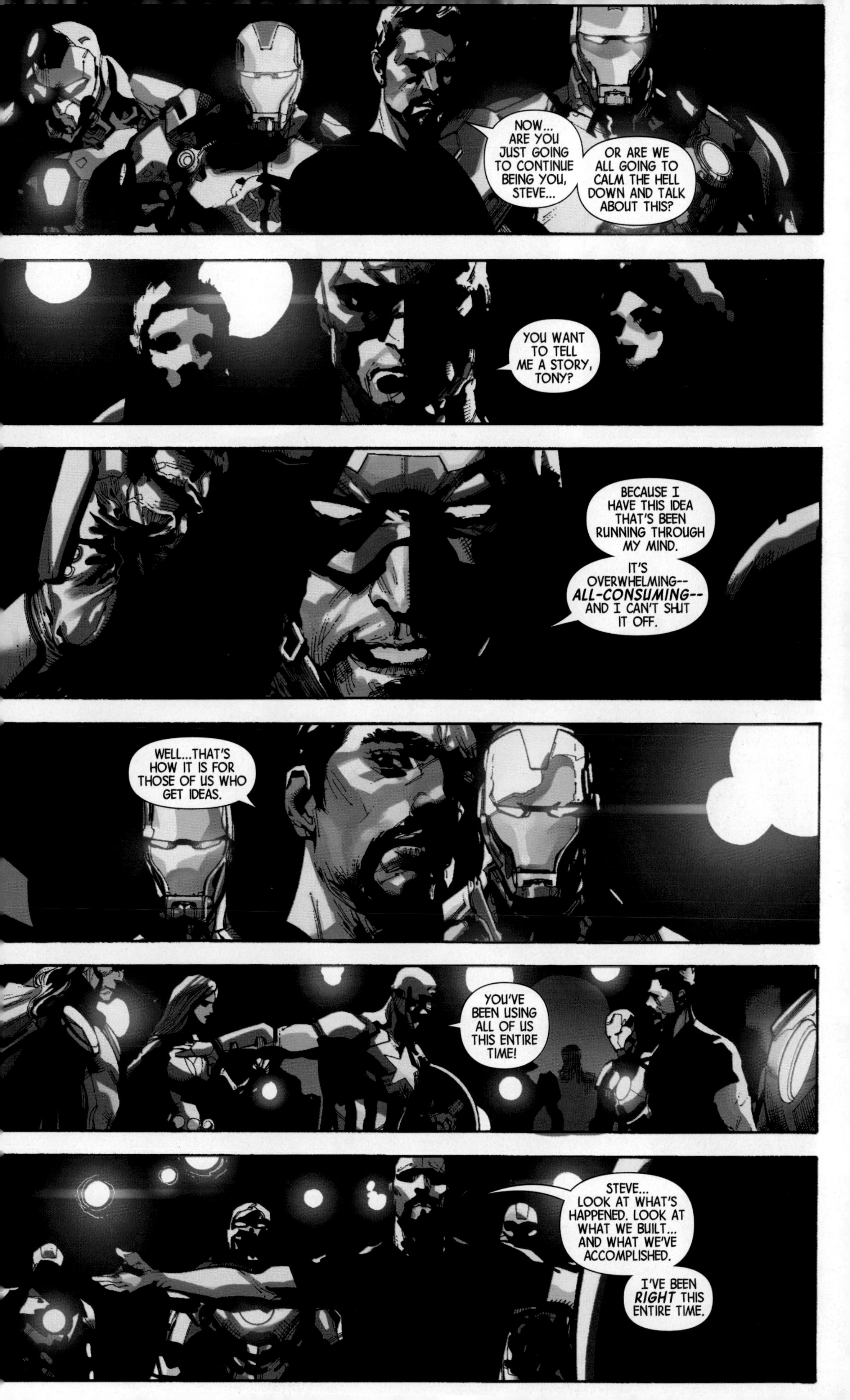

NOW... ARE YOU JUST GOING TO CONTINUE BEING YOU, STEVE...
OR ARE WE ALL GOING TO CALM THE HELL DOWN AND TALK ABOUT THIS?
YOU WANT TO TELL ME A STORY, TONY?
BECAUSE I HAVE THIS IDEA THAT'S BEEN RUNNING THROUGH MY MIND.
IT'S OVERWHELMING-- ALL-CONSUMING-- AND I CAN'T SHUT IT OFF.
WELL...THAT'S HOW IT IS FOR THOSE OF US WHO GET IDEAS.
YOU'VE BEEN USING ALL OF US THIS ENTIRE TIME!
STEVE... LOOK AT WHAT'S HAPPENED. LOOK AT WHAT WE BUILT... AND WHAT WE'VE ACCOMPLISHED.
I'VE BEEN RIGHT THIS ENTIRE TIME.

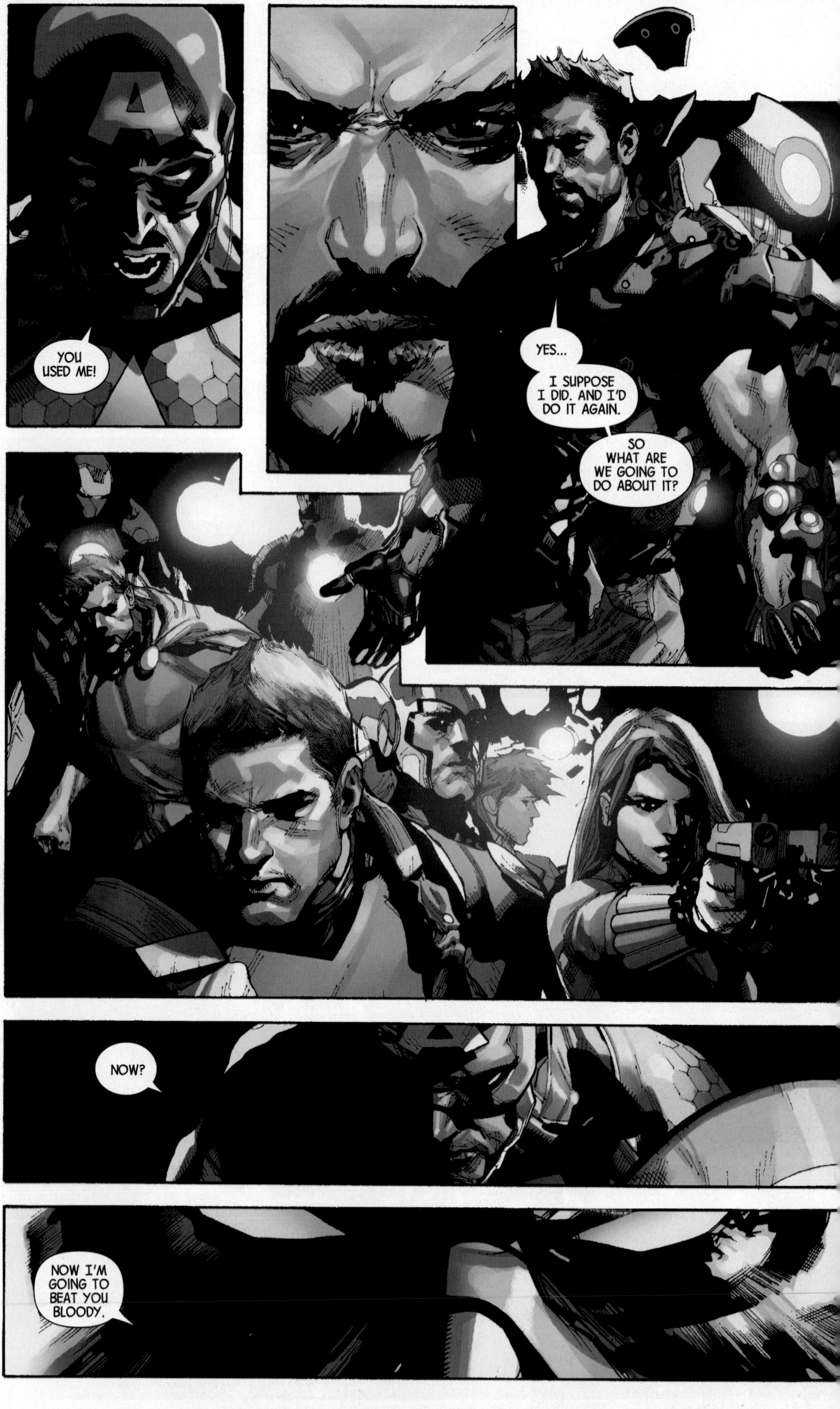
YOU USED ME!
YES...
I SUPPOSE I DID. AND I'D DO IT AGAIN.
SO WHAT ARE WE GOING TO DO ABOUT IT?
NOW?
NOW I'M GOING TO BEAT YOU BLOODY.

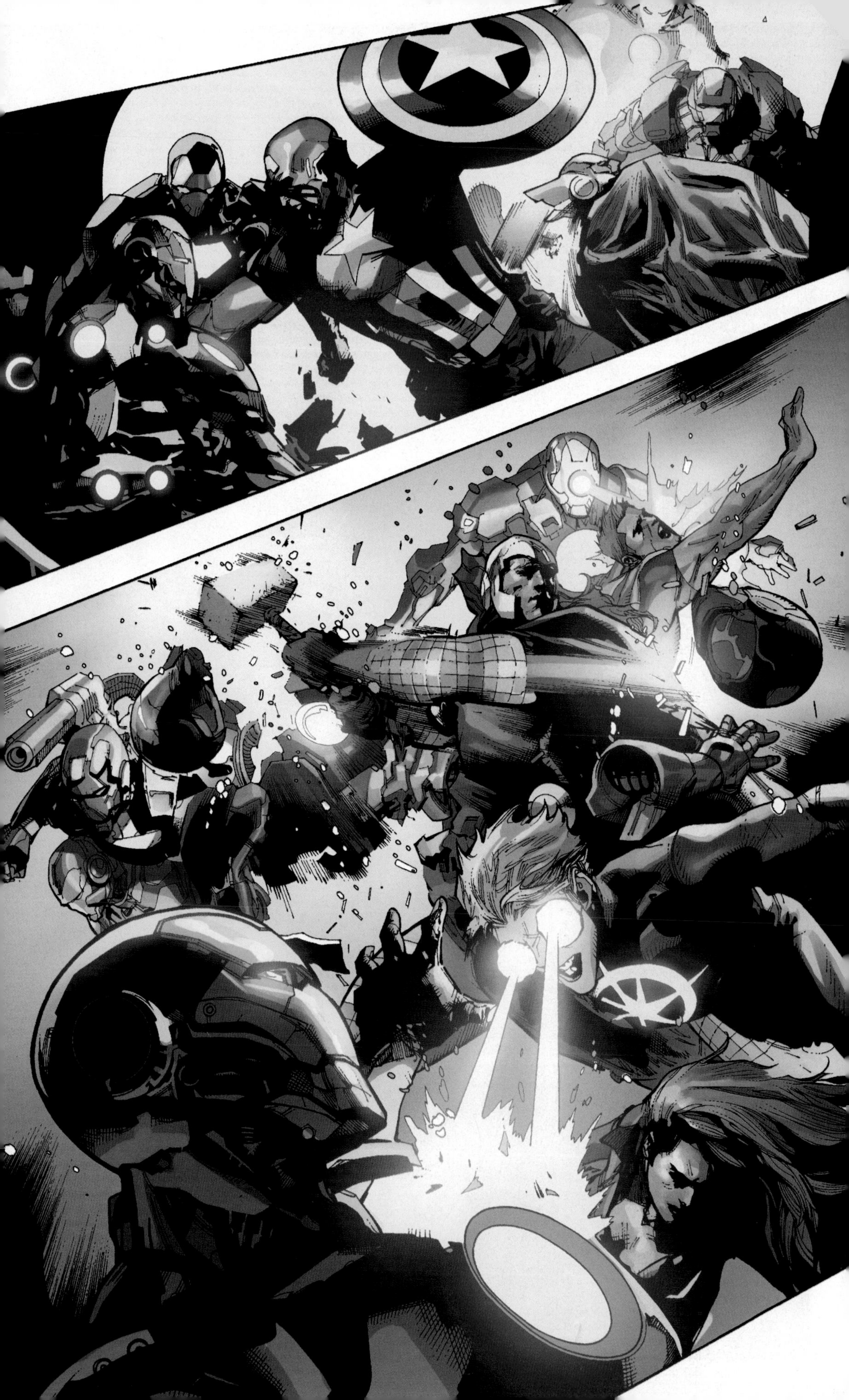

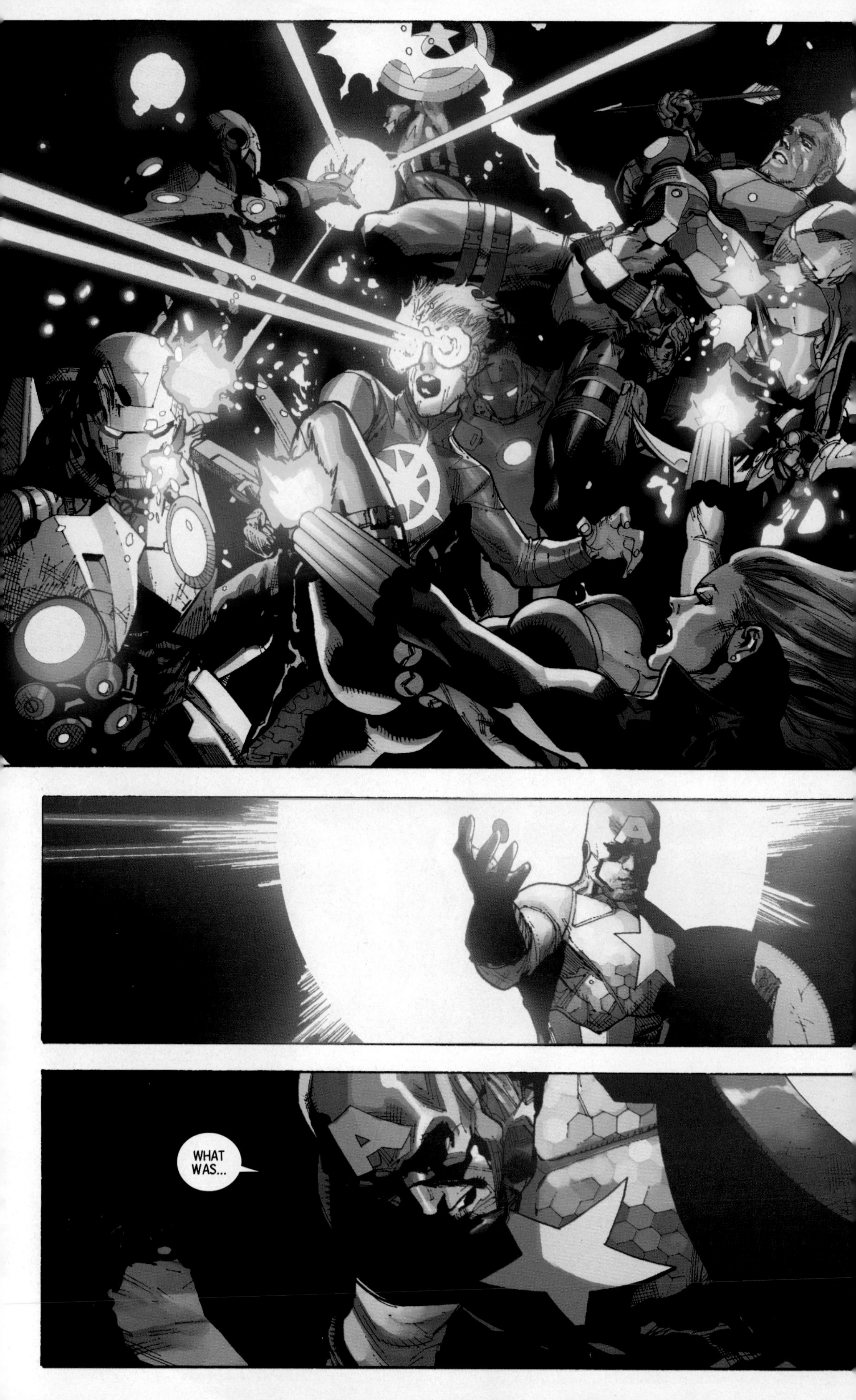
WHAT WAS...

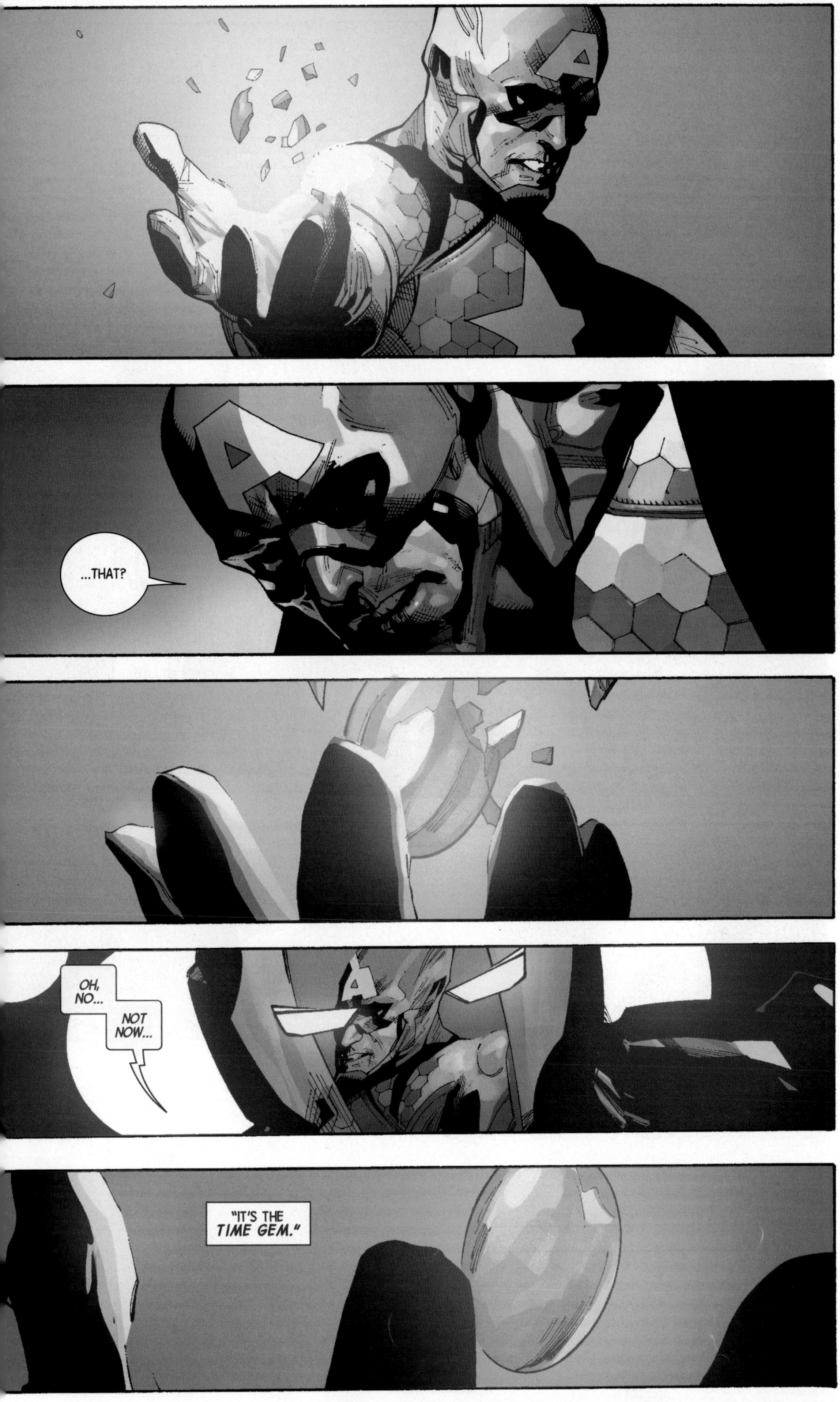
...THAT?
OH, NO...
NOT NOW...
"IT'S THE TIME GEM."

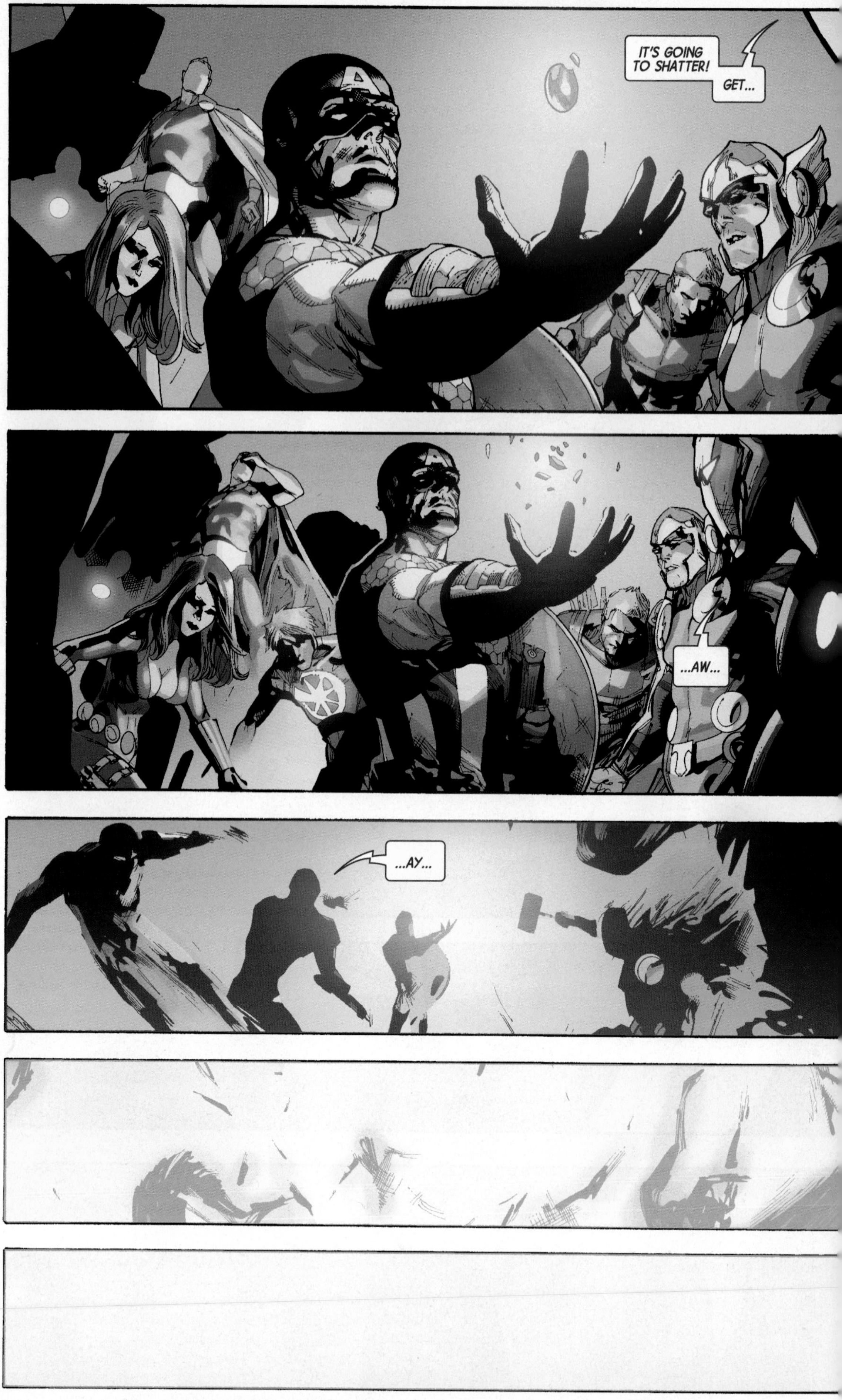
IT'S GOING TO SHATTER!
GET...
...AW...
...AY...

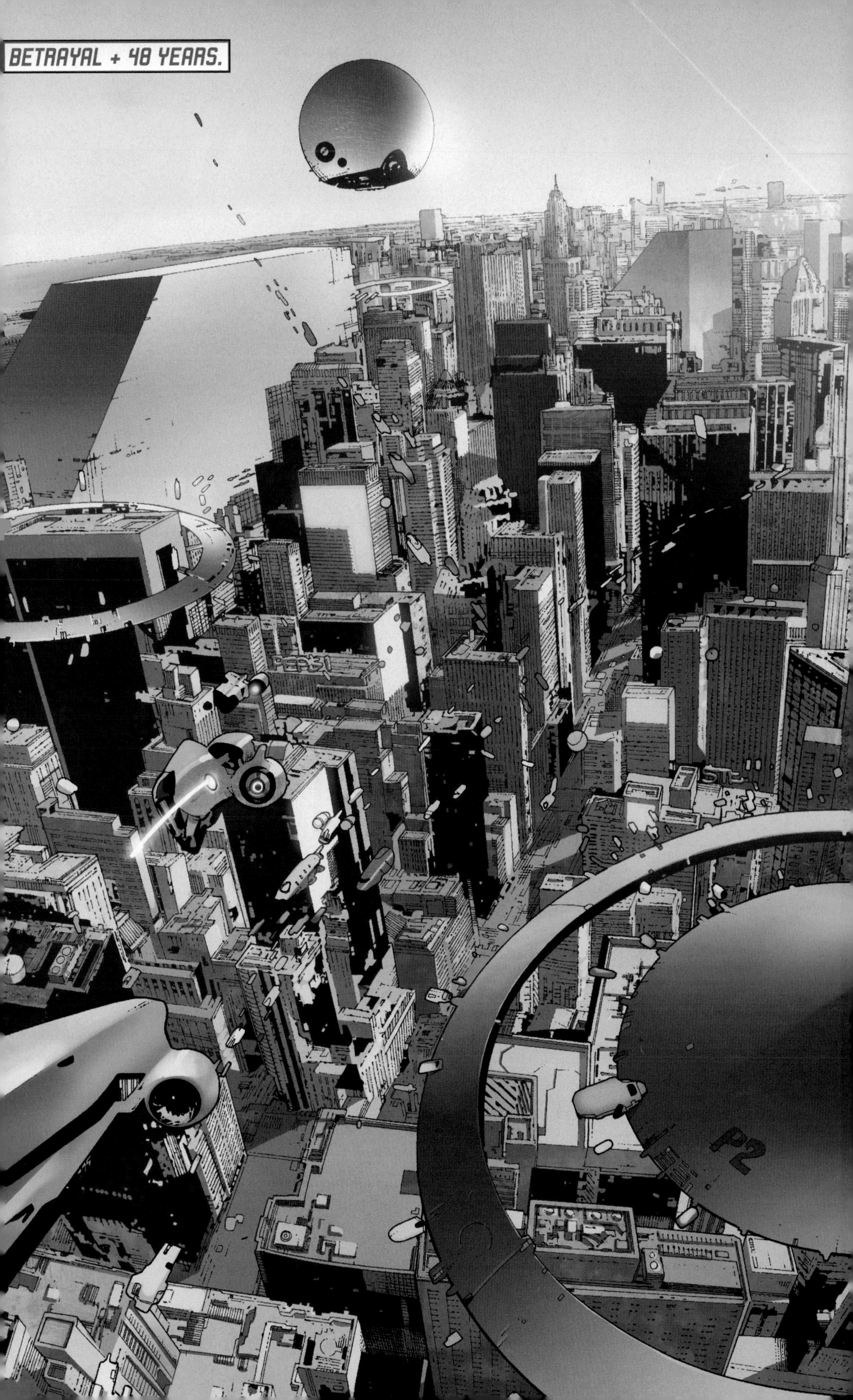
BETRAYAL + 48 YEARS.
P2

"FIFTY INTO THE FUTURE"

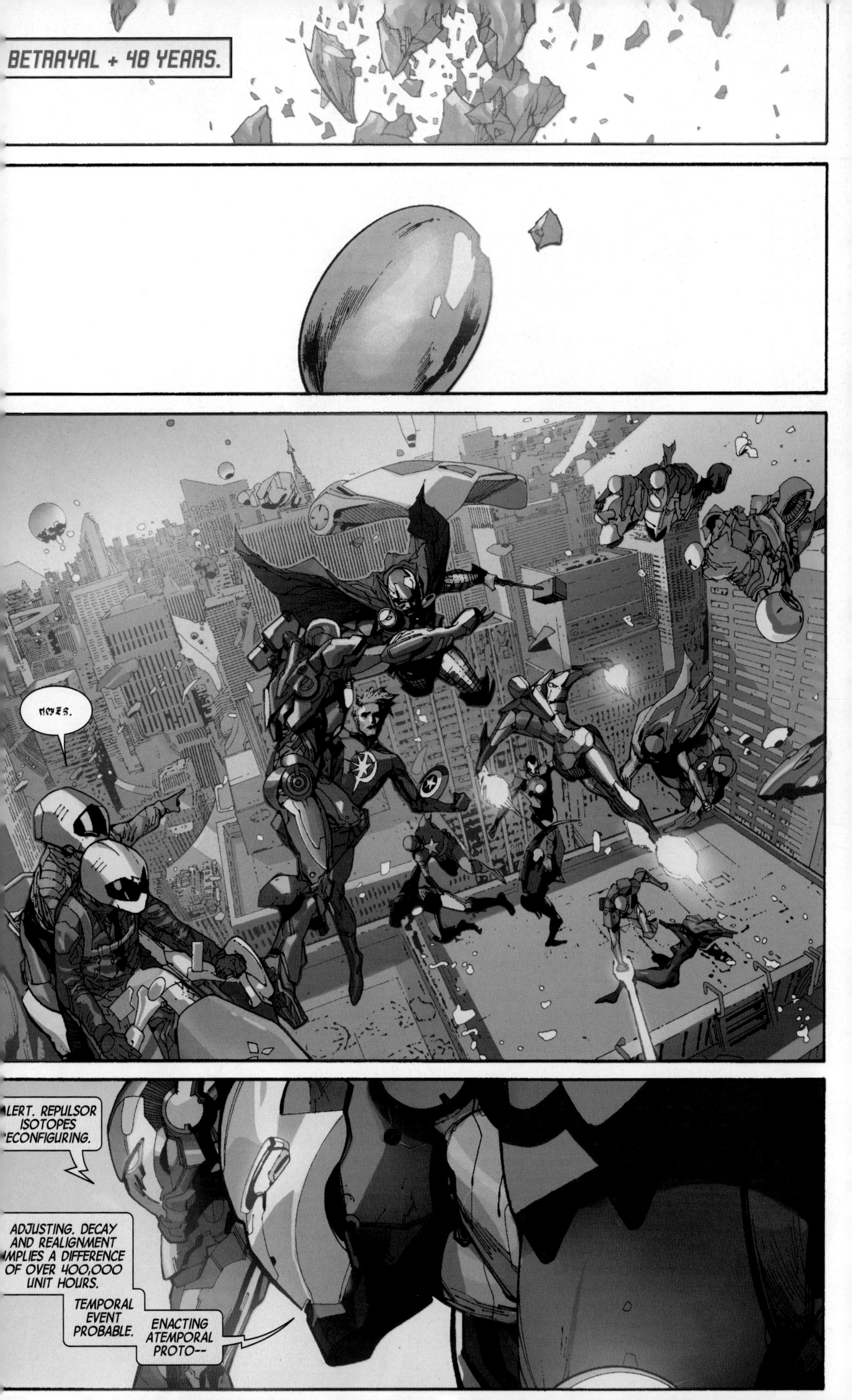
BETRAYAL + 48 YEARS.
LERT. REPULSOR ISOTOPES ECONFIGURING.
ADJUSTING. DECAY AND REALIGNMENT MPLIES A DIFFERENCE OF OVER 400,000 UNIT HOURS.
TEMPORAL EVENT PROBABLE.
ENACTING ATEMPORAL PROTO--

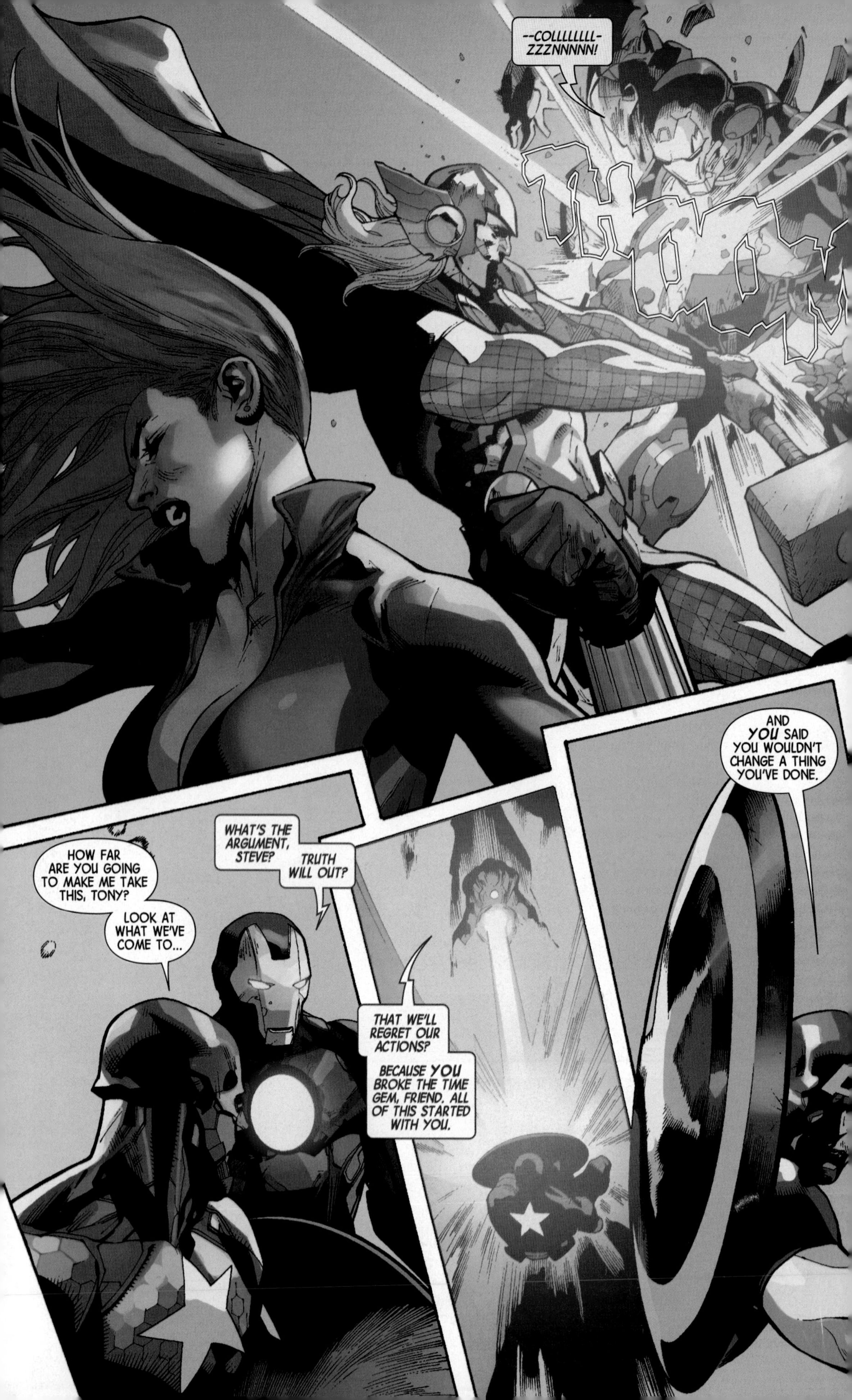

--COLLLLLLLL-ZZZNNNNN!
WHOOOM
HOW FAR ARE YOU GOING TO MAKE ME TAKE THIS, TONY?
LOOK AT WHAT WE'VE COME TO...
WHAT'S THE ARGUMENT, STEVE?
TRUTH WILL OUT?
THAT WE'LL REGRET OUR ACTIONS?
BECAUSE YOU BROKE THE TIME GEM, FRIEND. ALL OF THIS STARTED WITH YOU.
AND YOU SAID YOU WOULDN'T CHANGE A THING YOU'VE DONE.

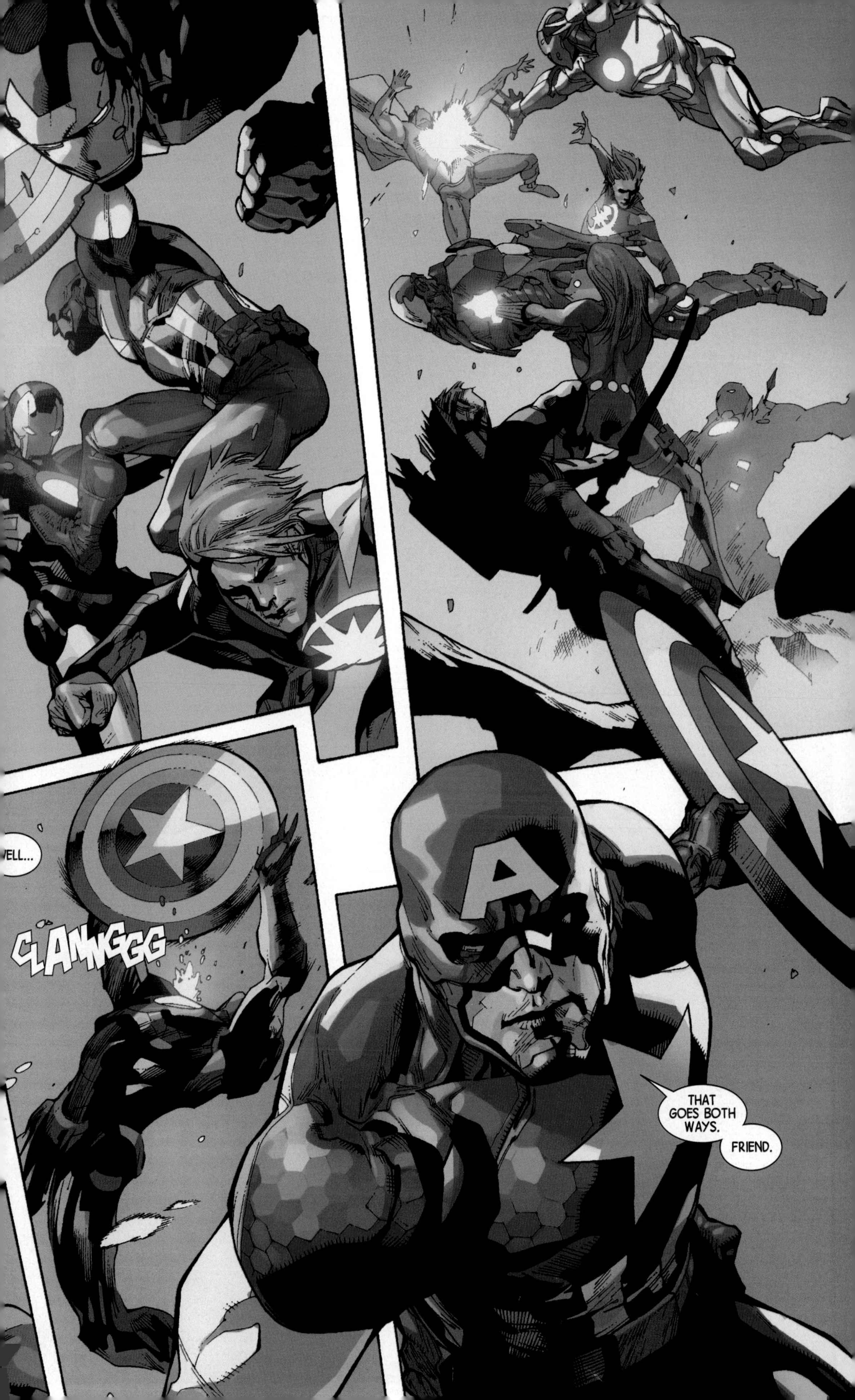

ELL...
CLANNGGG
THAT GOES BOTH WAYS.
FRIEND.

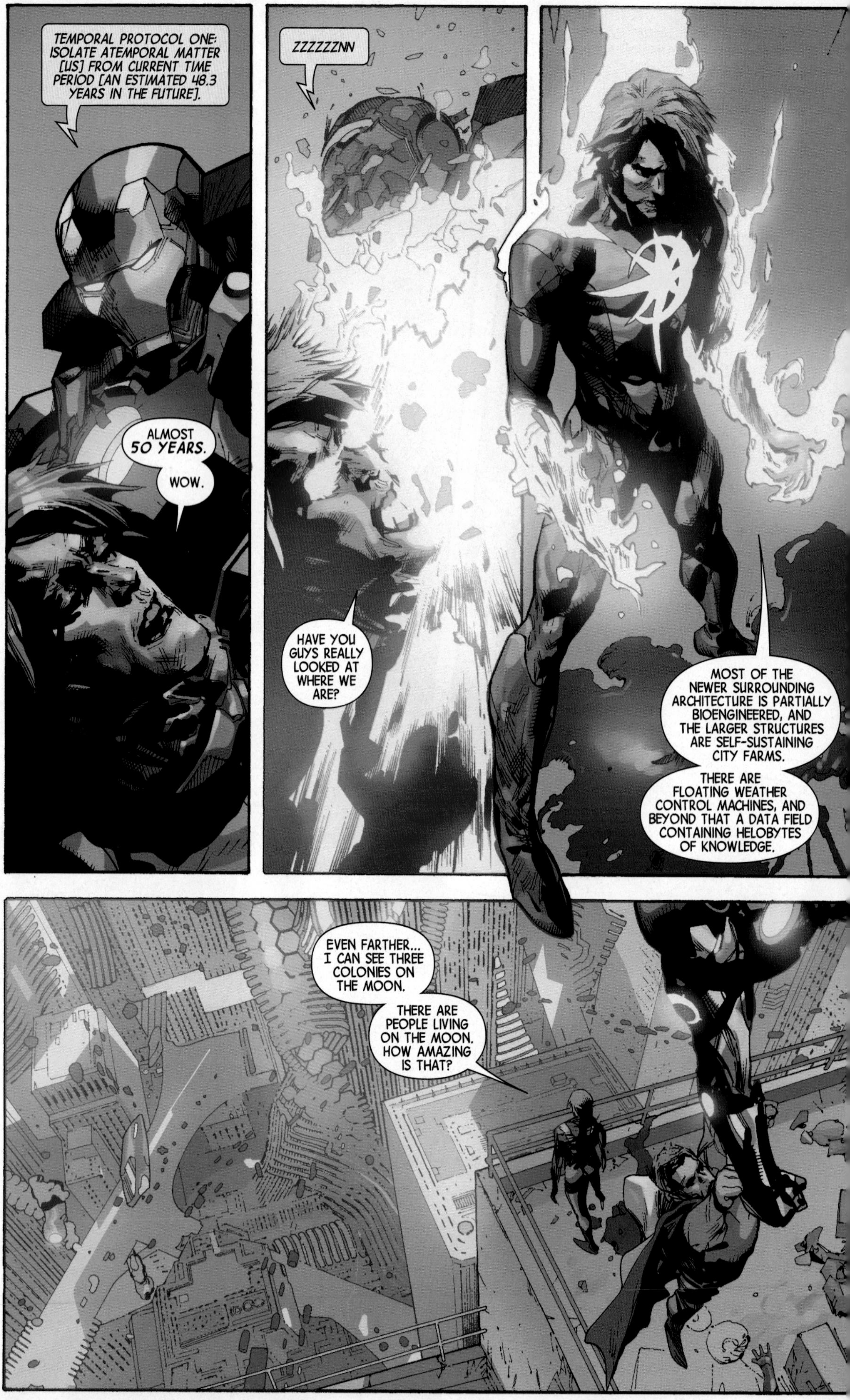
TEMPORAL PROTOCOL ONE: ISOLATE ATEMPORAL MATTER [US] FROM CURRENT TIME PERIOD [AN ESTIMATED 48.3 YEARS IN THE FUTURE].
ALMOST 50 YEARS.
WOW.
ZZZZZZNN
HAVE YOU GUYS REALLY LOOKED AT WHERE WE ARE?
MOST OF THE NEWER SURROUNDING ARCHITECTURE IS PARTIALLY BIOENGINEERED, AND THE LARGER STRUCTURES ARE SELF-SUSTAINING CITY FARMS.
THERE ARE FLOATING WEATHER CONTROL MACHINES, AND BEYOND THAT A DATA FIELD CONTAINING HELOBYTES OF KNOWLEDGE.
EVEN FARTHER... I CAN SEE THREE COLONIES ON THE MOON.
THERE ARE PEOPLE LIVING ON THE MOON. HOW AMAZING IS THAT?

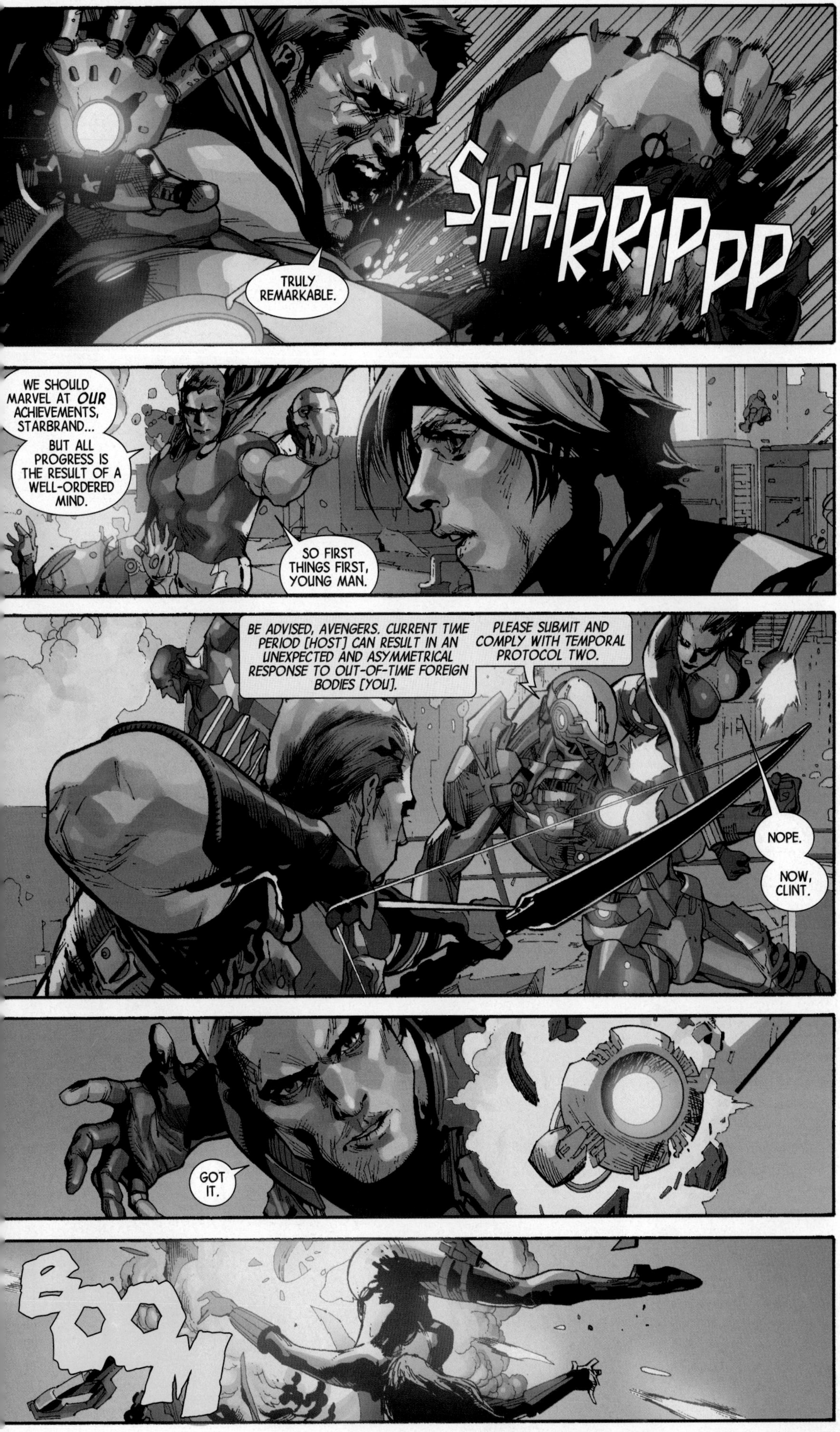
SHHRRIPPP
TRULY REMARKABLE.
WE SHOULD MARVEL AT OUR ACHIEVEMENTS, STARBRAND...
BUT ALL PROGRESS IS THE RESULT OF A WELL-ORDERED MIND.
SO FIRST THINGS FIRST, YOUNG MAN.
BE ADVISED, AVENGERS. CURRENT TIME PERIOD [HOST] CAN RESULT IN AN UNEXPECTED AND ASYMMETRICAL RESPONSE TO OUT-OF-TIME FOREIGN BODIES [YOU].
PLEASE SUBMIT AND COMPLY WITH TEMPORAL PROTOCOL TWO.
NOPE.
NOW, CLINT.
GOT IT.
BOOM

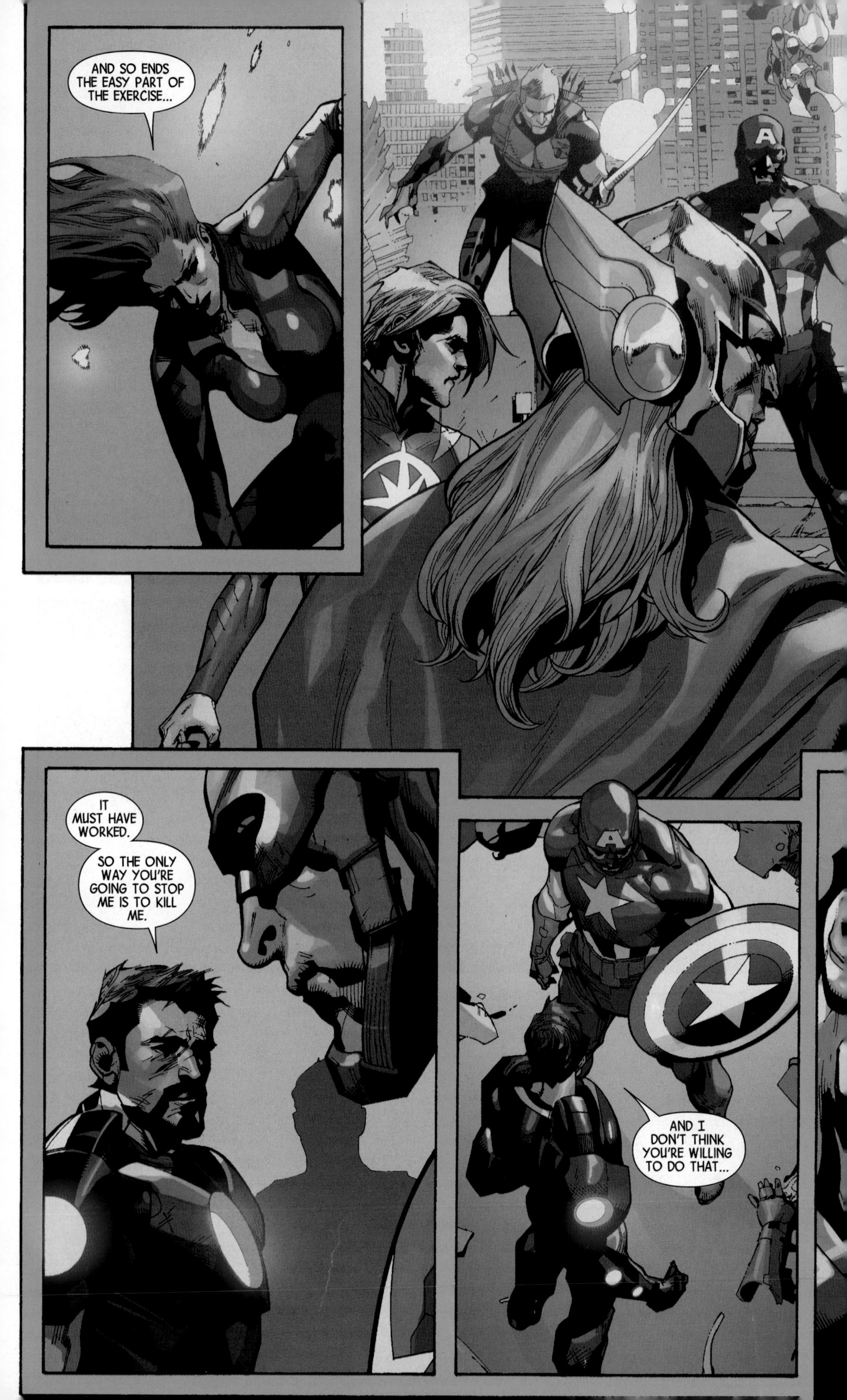
AND SO ENDS THE EASY PART OF THE EXERCISE...
IT MUST HAVE WORKED.
SO THE ONLY WAY YOU'RE GOING TO STOP ME IS TO KILL ME.
AND I DON'T THINK YOU'RE WILLING TO DO THAT...

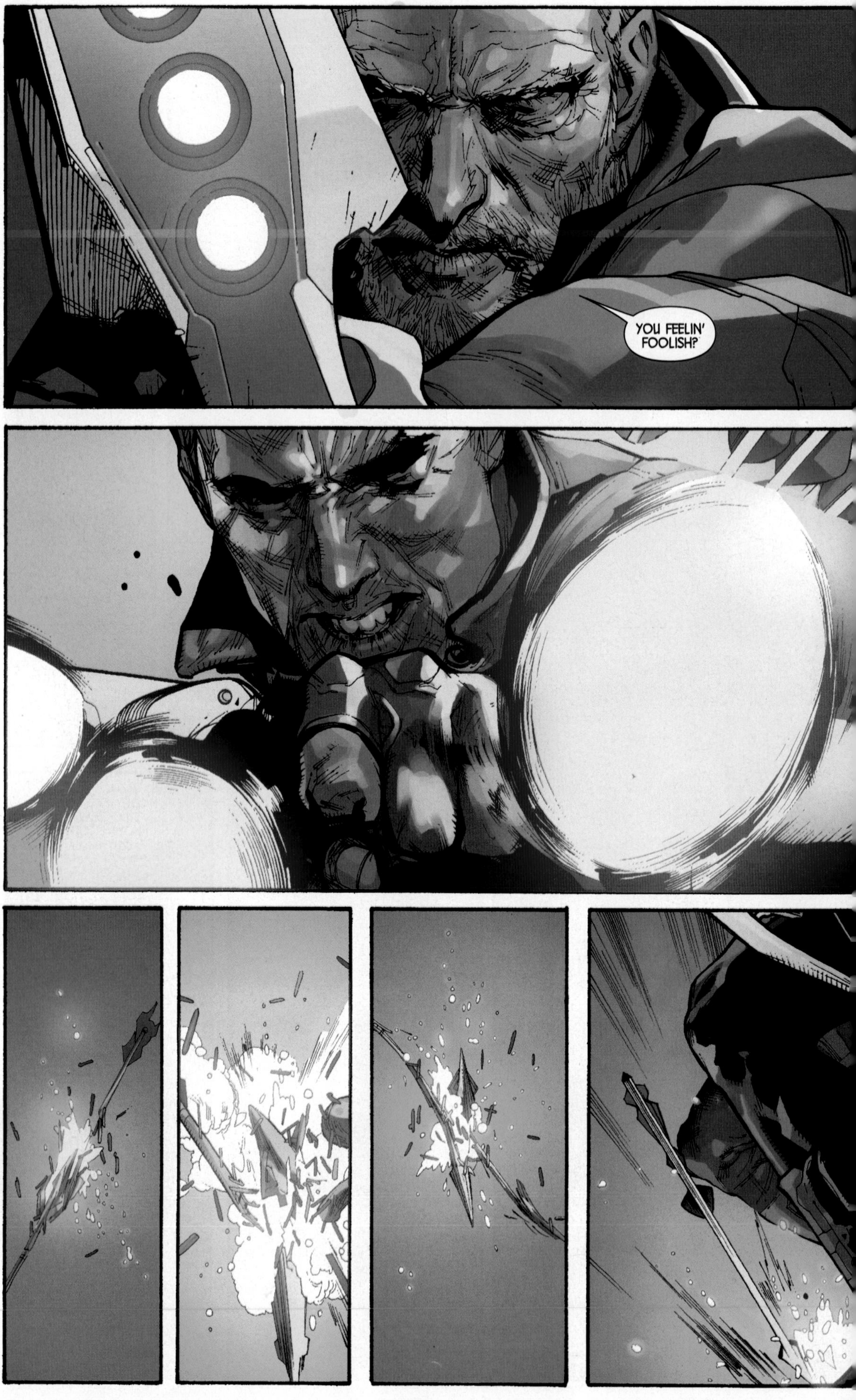
YOU FEELIN' FOOLISH?

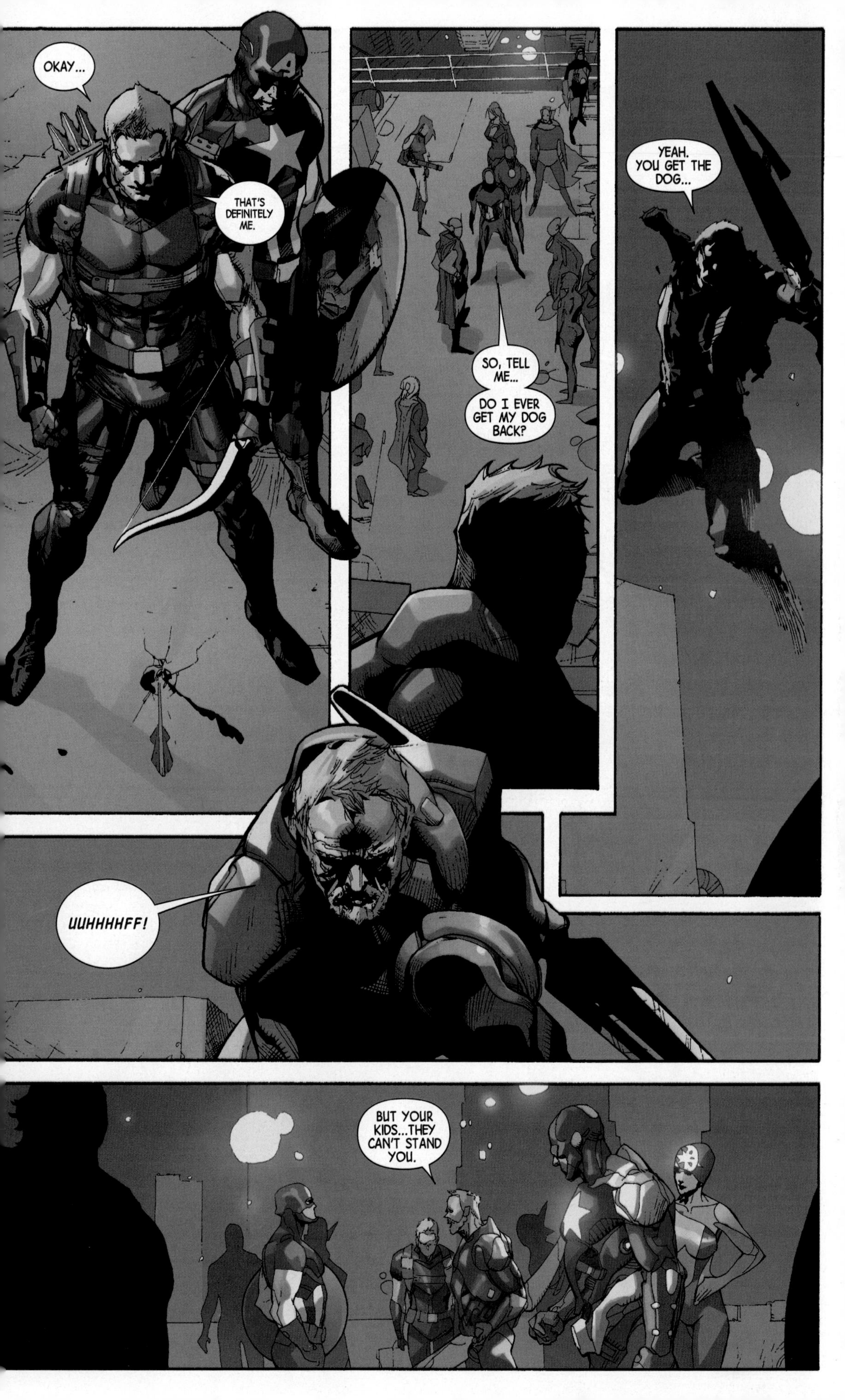
OKAY...
THAT'S DEFINITELY ME.
SO, TELL ME...
DO I EVER GET MY DOG BACK?
YEAH. YOU GET THE DOG...
UUHHHHFF!
BUT YOUR KIDS...THEY CAN'T STAND YOU.

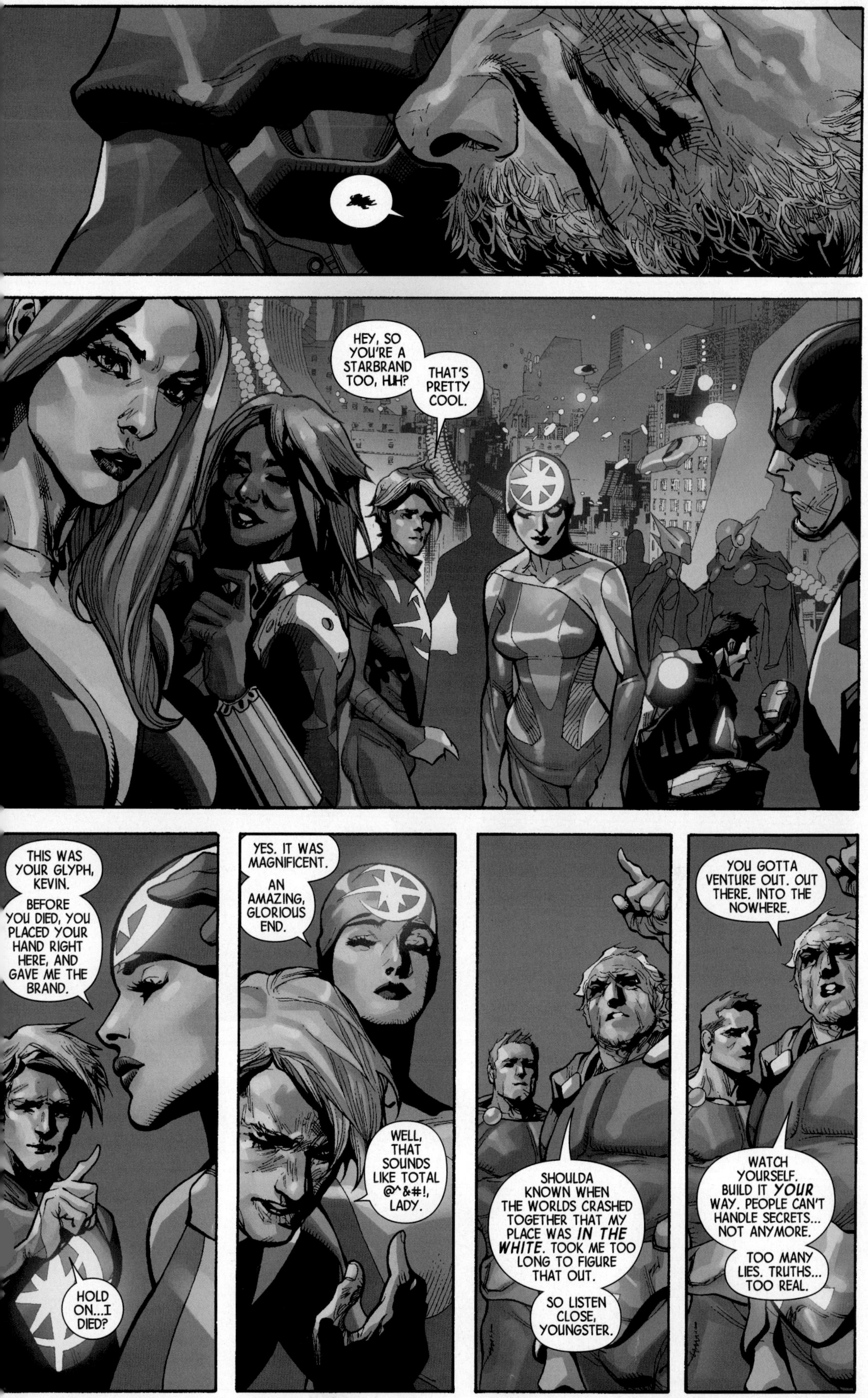

HEY, SO YOU'RE A STARBRAND TOO, HUH?
THAT'S PRETTY COOL.
THIS WAS YOUR GLYPH, KEVIN.
BEFORE YOU DIED, YOU PLACED YOUR HAND RIGHT HERE, AND GAVE ME THE BRAND.
HOLD ON...I DIED?
YES. IT WAS MAGNIFICENT.
AN AMAZING, GLORIOUS END.
WELL, THAT SOUNDS LIKE TOTAL @^&#!, LADY.
SHOULDA KNOWN WHEN THE WORLDS CRASHED TOGETHER THAT MY PLACE WAS *IN THE WHITE*. TOOK ME TOO LONG TO FIGURE THAT OUT.
SO LISTEN CLOSE, YOUNGSTER.
YOU GOTTA VENTURE OUT. OUT THERE. INTO THE NOWHERE.
WATCH YOURSELF. BUILD IT *YOUR* WAY. PEOPLE CAN'T HANDLE SECRETS... NOT ANYMORE.
TOO MANY LIES. TRUTHS... TOO REAL.

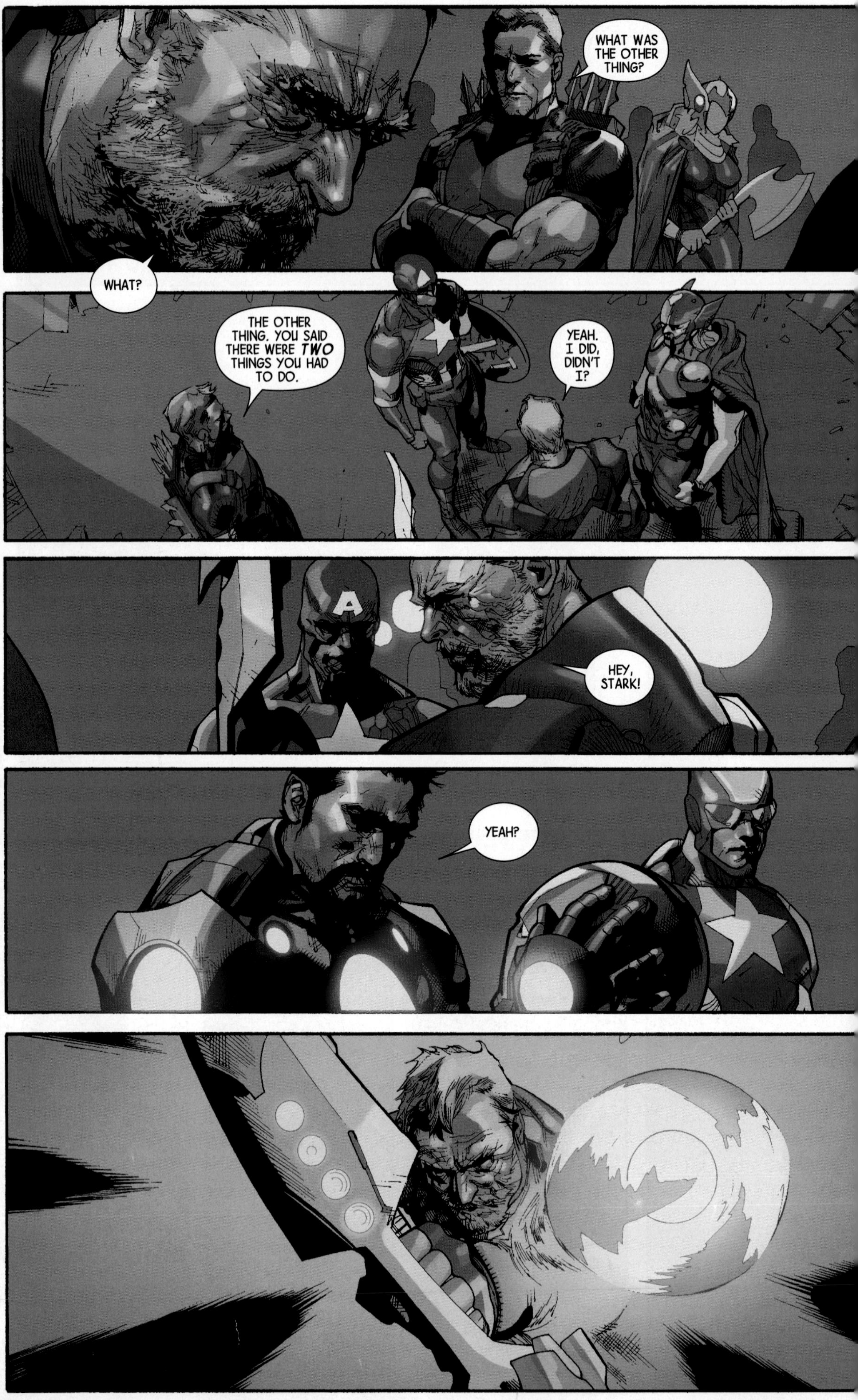
WHAT WAS THE OTHER THING?
WHAT?
THE OTHER THING. YOU SAID THERE WERE *TWO* THINGS YOU HAD TO DO.
YEAH. I DID, DIDN'T I?
HEY, STARK!
YEAH?

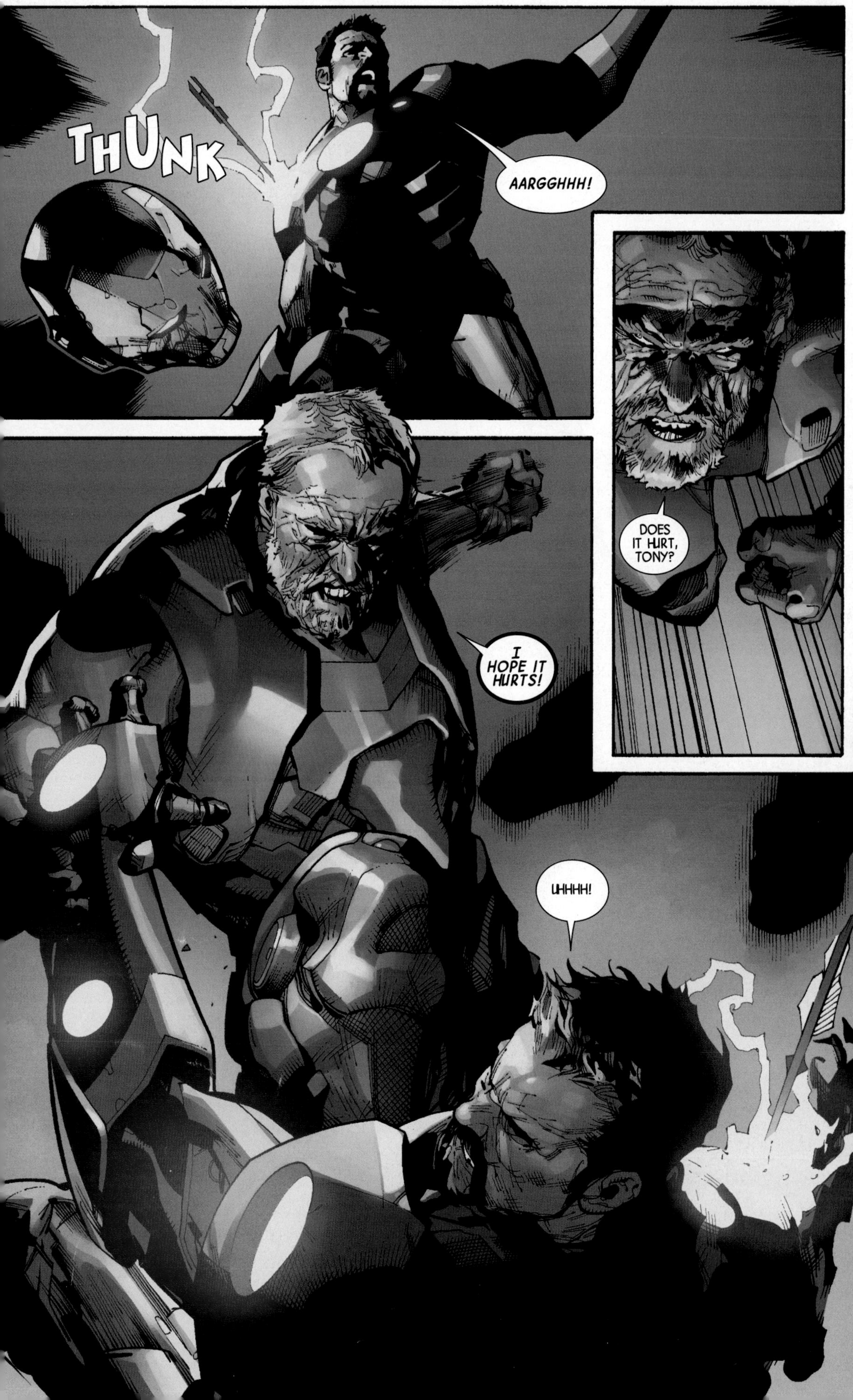
THUNK
AARGGHHH!
DOES IT HURT, TONY?
I HOPE IT HURTS!
UHHHH!

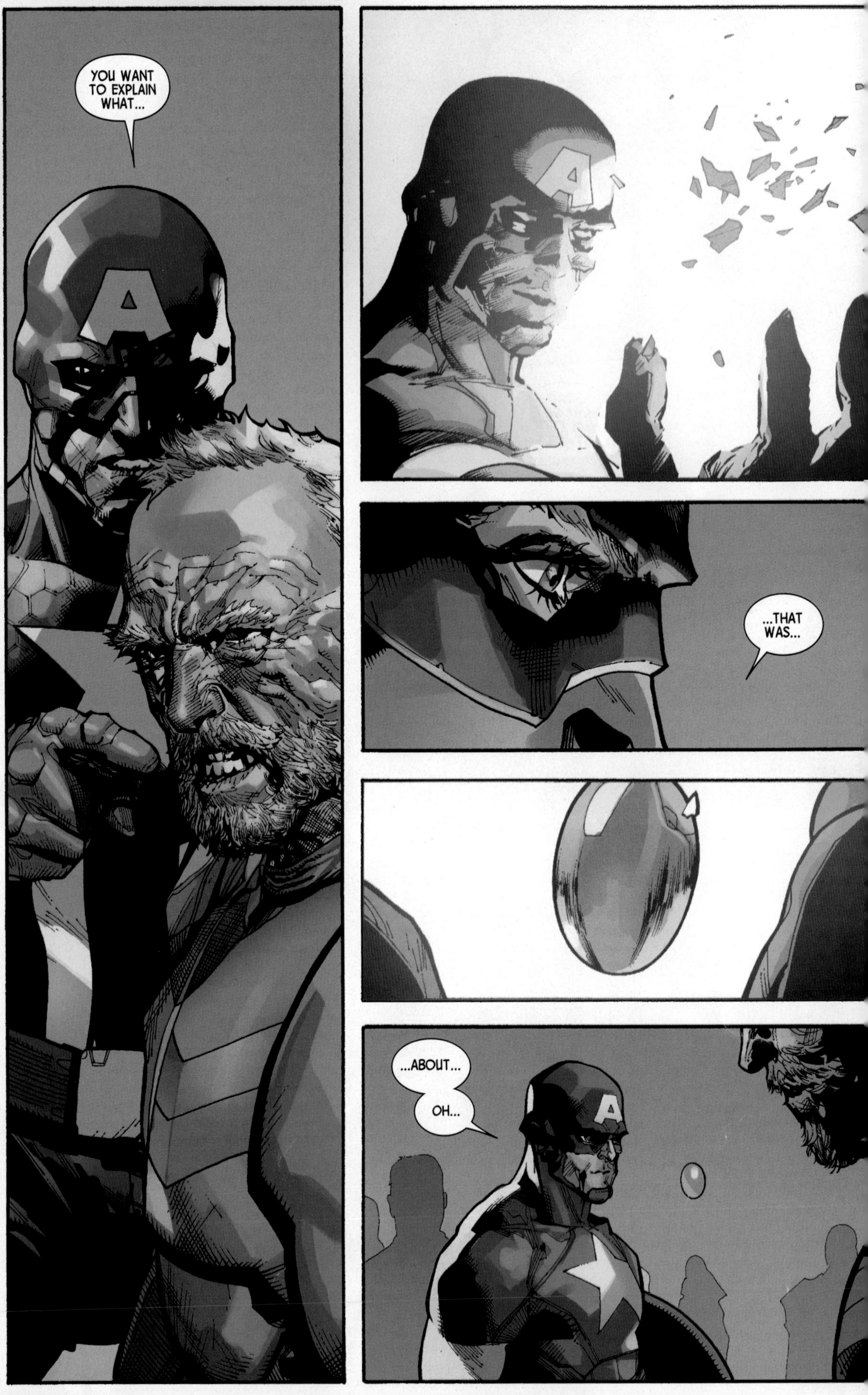
YOU WANT TO EXPLAIN WHAT...
...THAT WAS...
...ABOUT...
OH...

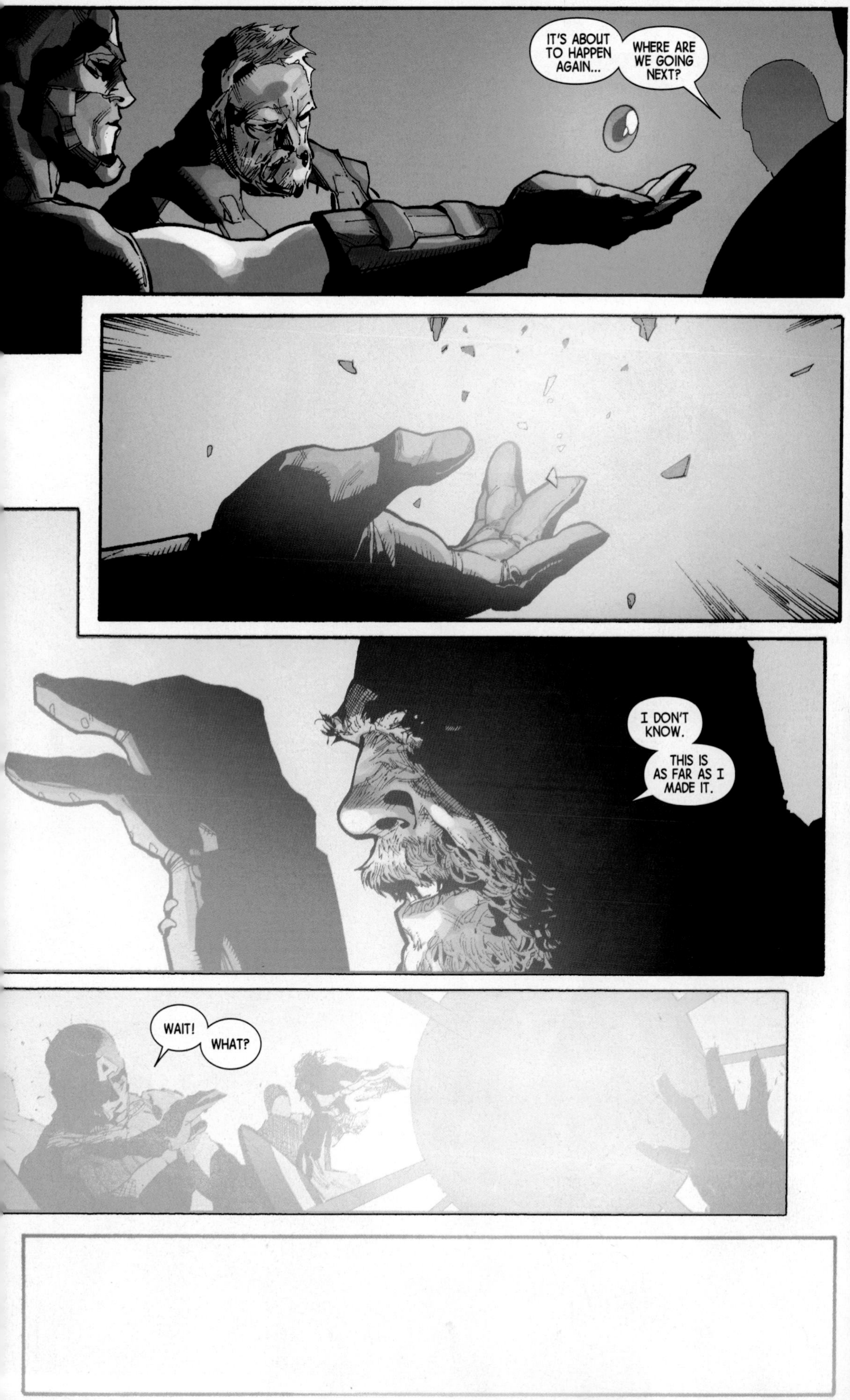
IT'S ABOUT TO HAPPEN AGAIN...
WHERE ARE WE GOING NEXT?
I DON'T KNOW.
THIS IS AS FAR AS I MADE IT.
WAIT!
WHAT?

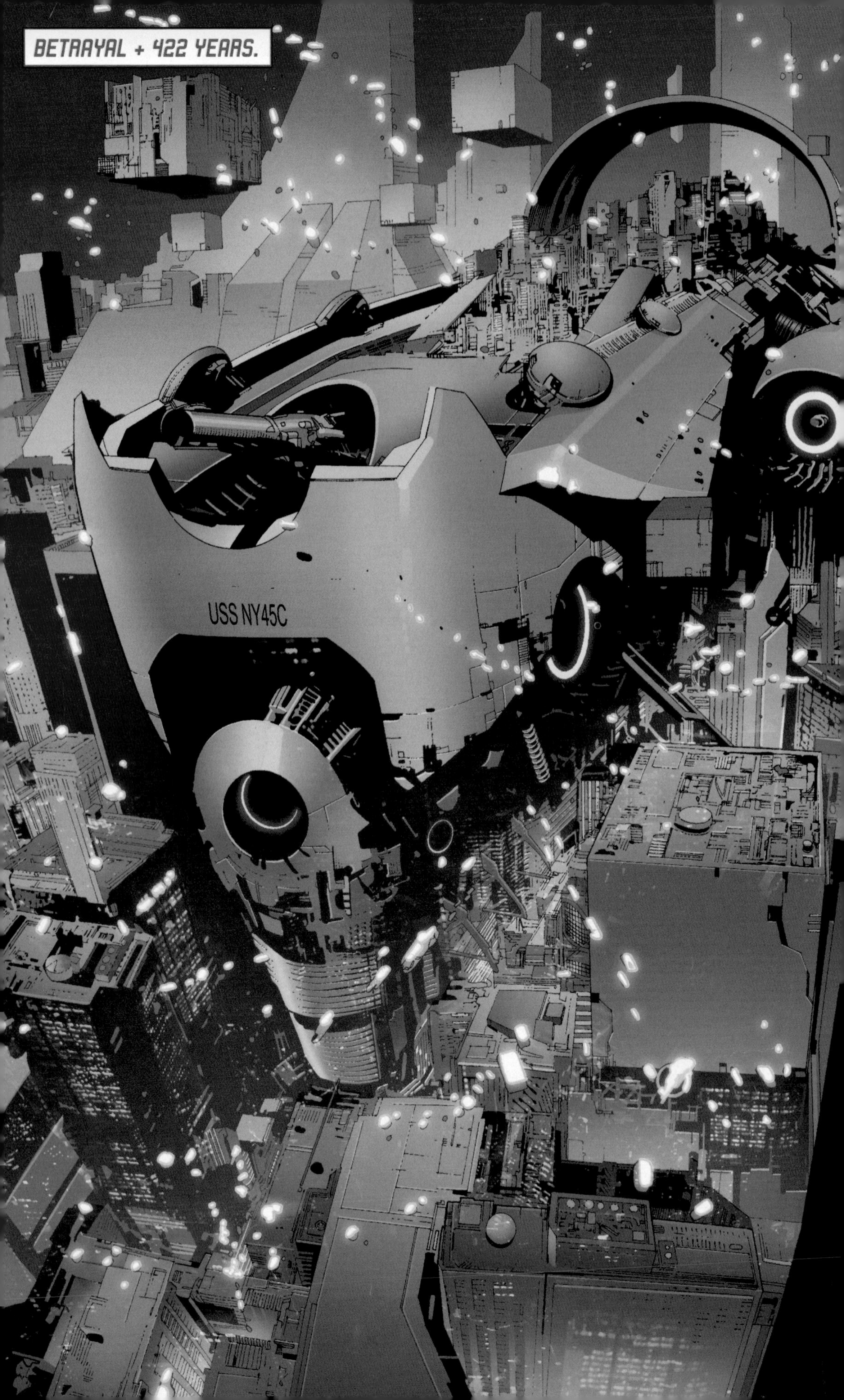
BETRAYAL + 422 YEARS.
USS NY45C

"500 INTO THE FUTURE"

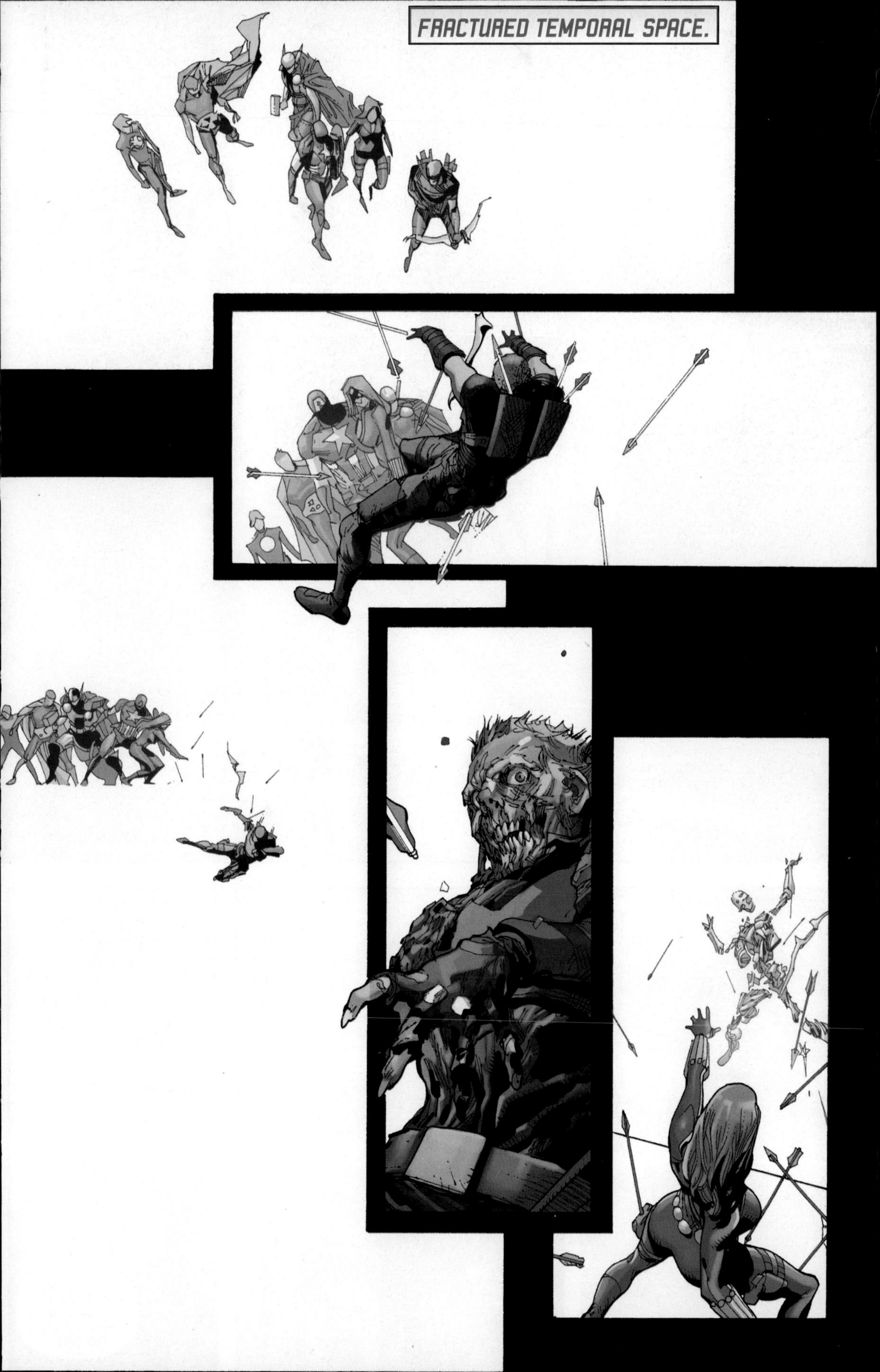
FRACTURED TEMPORAL SPACE.

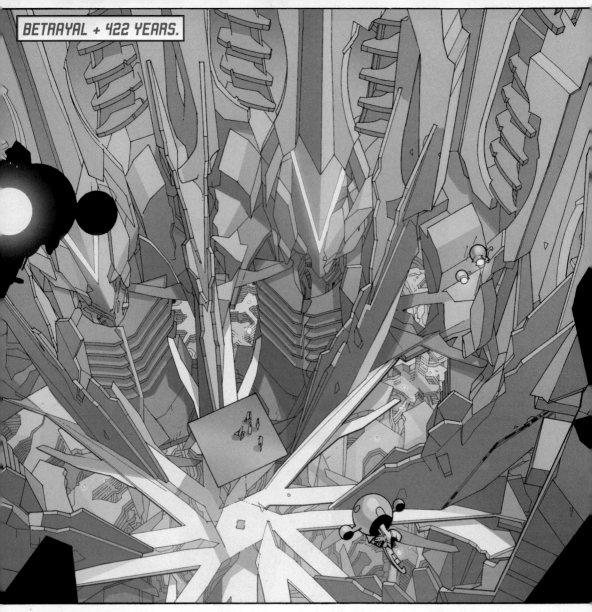

YOU ALL SAW THAT, DIDN'T YOU?

HAWKEYE JUST FADED AWAY, RIGHT BEFORE OUR EYES.

YEAH.

DO YOU THINK--?

DEAD? NO...

128-234-871-982-009-228-843-091

I HEARD OLD MAN BARTON SAY HE DIDN'T GO ANY FURTHER INTO THE FUTURE...

WHICH MEANS HE REMEMBERED... AND MUST HAVE LIVED TO TELL THE TALE...

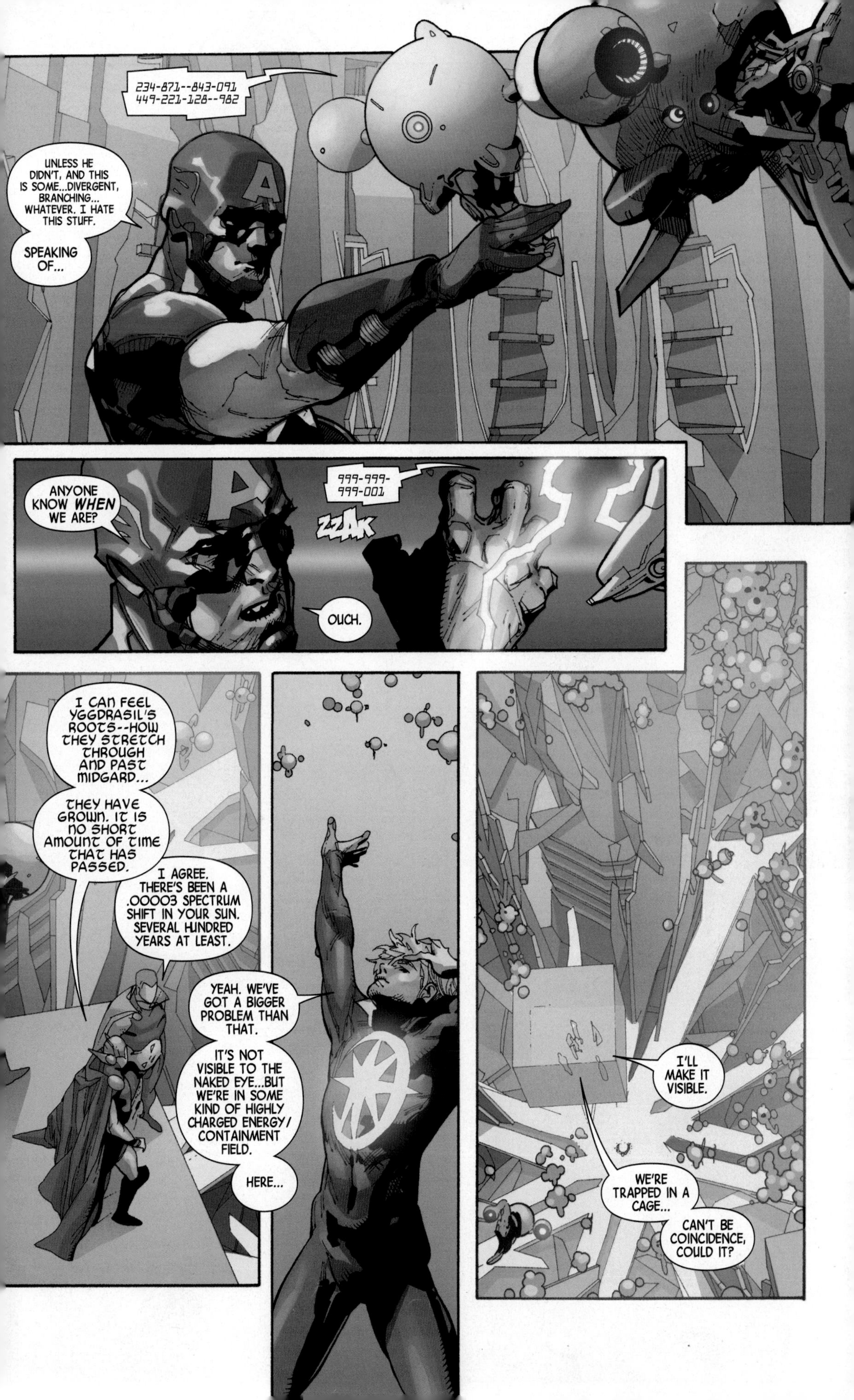
234-871--843-091
449-221-128--982
UNLESS HE DIDN'T, AND THIS IS SOME...DIVERGENT, BRANCHING... WHATEVER. I HATE THIS STUFF.
SPEAKING OF...
ANYONE KNOW WHEN WE ARE?
999-999-999-001
ZZAK
OUCH.
I CAN FEEL YGGDRASIL'S ROOTS--HOW THEY STRETCH THROUGH AND PAST MIDGARD...
THEY HAVE GROWN. IT IS NO SHORT AMOUNT OF TIME THAT HAS PASSED.
I AGREE. THERE'S BEEN A .00003 SPECTRUM SHIFT IN YOUR SUN. SEVERAL HUNDRED YEARS AT LEAST.
YEAH. WE'VE GOT A BIGGER PROBLEM THAN THAT.
IT'S NOT VISIBLE TO THE NAKED EYE...BUT WE'RE IN SOME KIND OF HIGHLY CHARGED ENERGY/ CONTAINMENT FIELD.
HERE...
I'LL MAKE IT VISIBLE.
WE'RE TRAPPED IN A CAGE...
CAN'T BE COINCIDENCE, COULD IT?

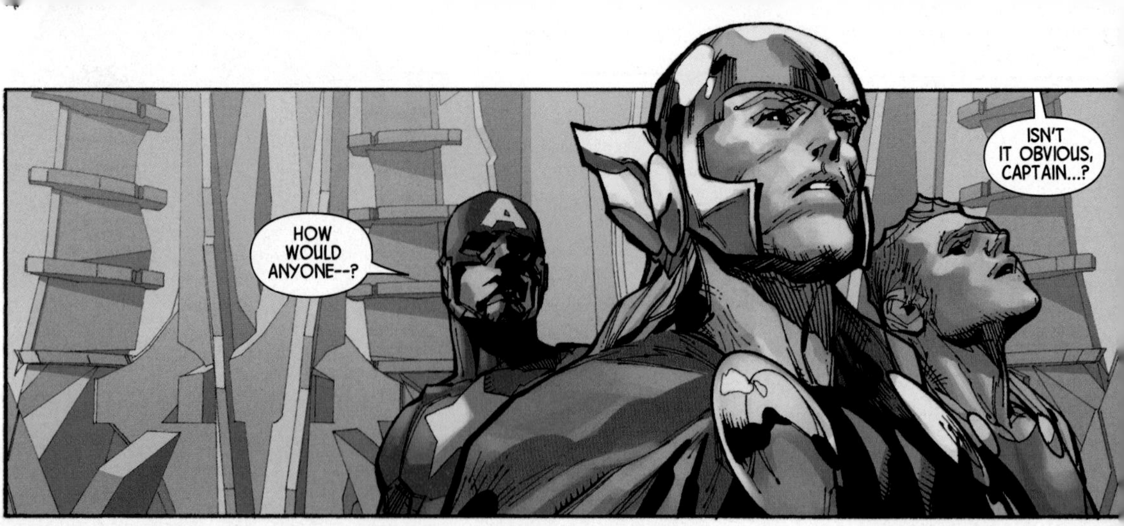
HOW WOULD ANYONE--?
ISN'T IT OBVIOUS, CAPTAIN...?

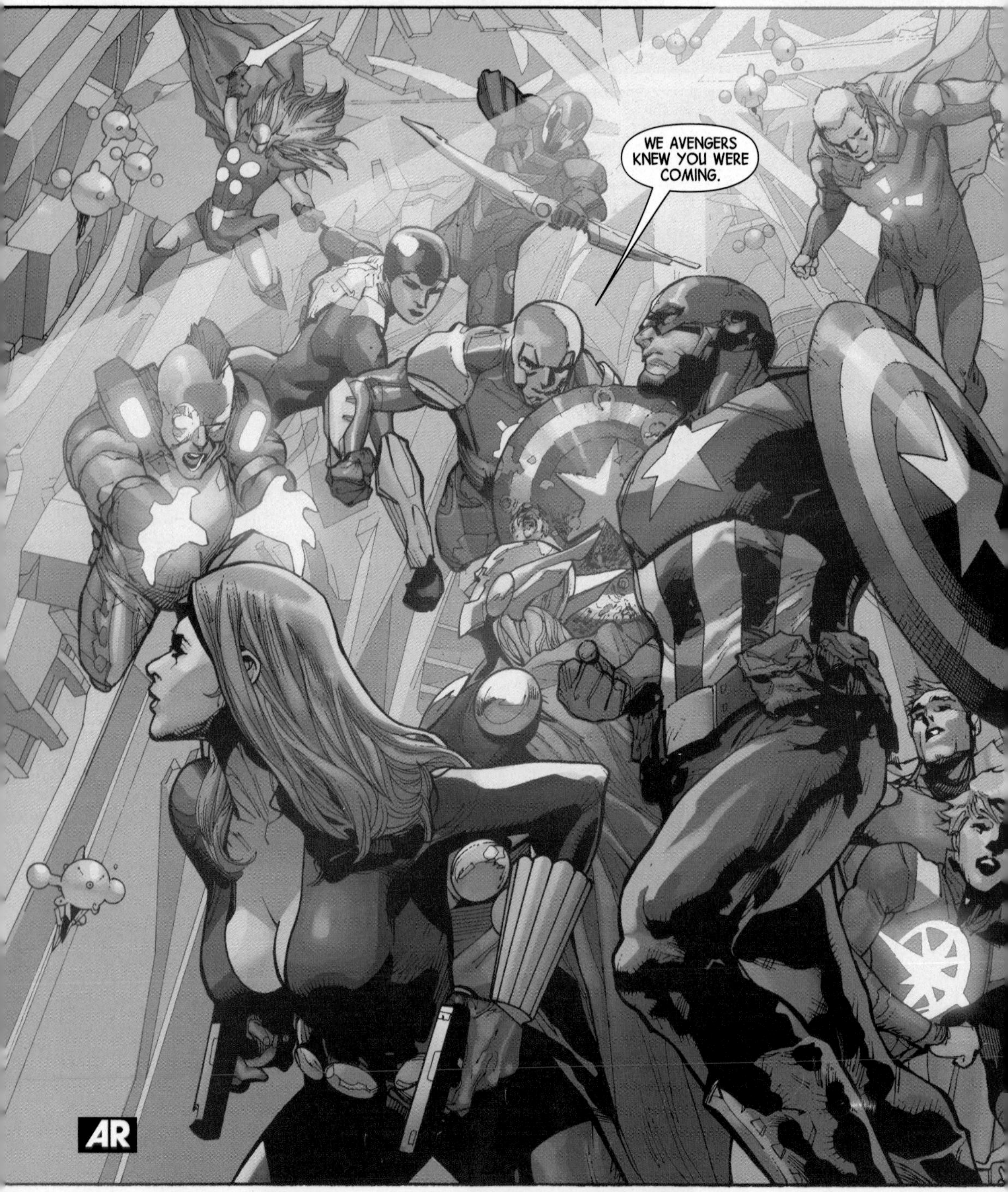
WE AVENGERS KNEW YOU WERE COMING.

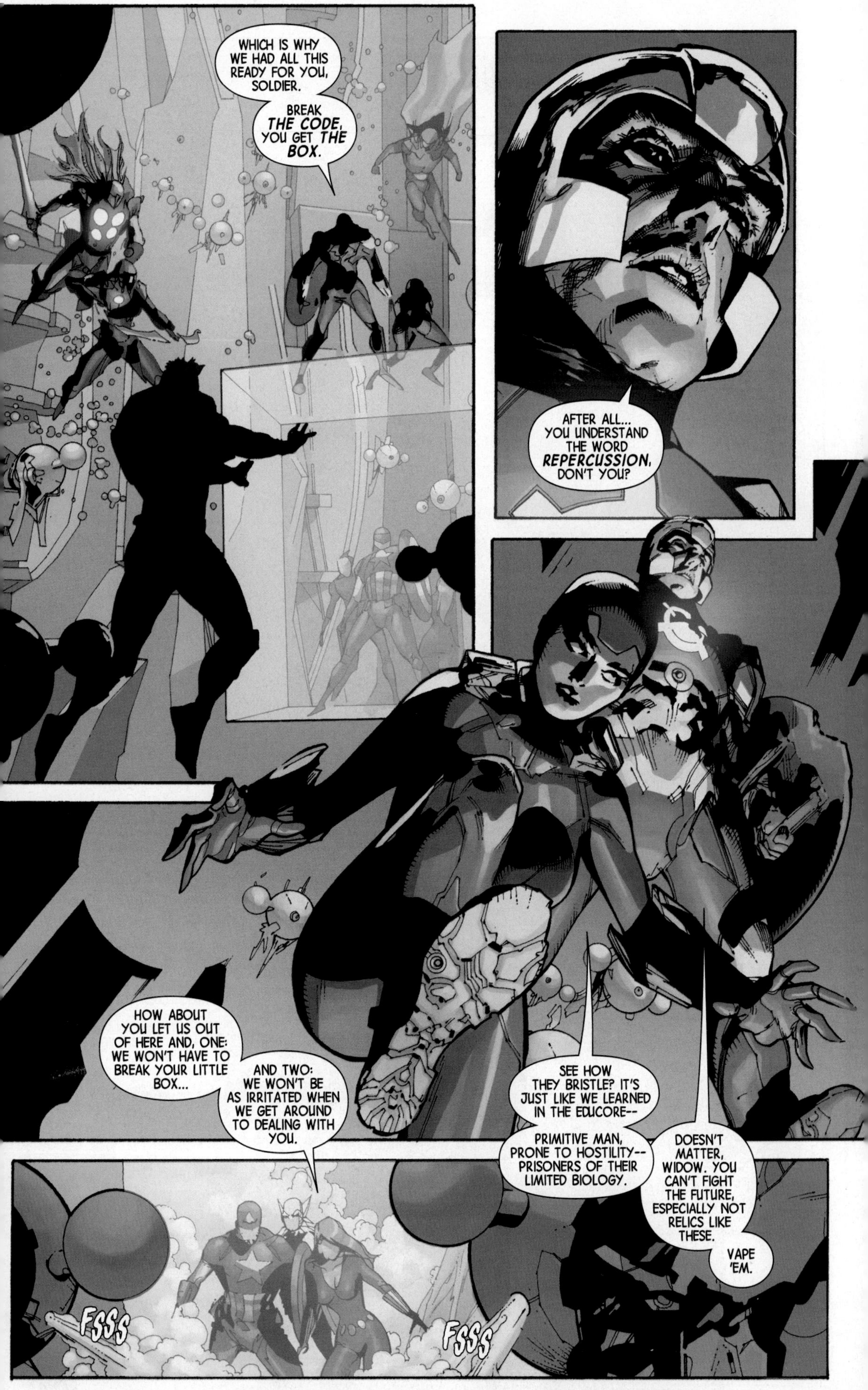
WHICH IS WHY WE HAD ALL THIS READY FOR YOU, SOLDIER.
BREAK *THE CODE*, YOU GET *THE BOX*.
AFTER ALL... YOU UNDERSTAND THE WORD *REPERCUSSION*, DON'T YOU?
HOW ABOUT YOU LET US OUT OF HERE AND, ONE: WE WON'T HAVE TO BREAK YOUR LITTLE BOX...
AND TWO: WE WON'T BE AS IRRITATED WHEN WE GET AROUND TO DEALING WITH YOU.
SEE HOW THEY BRISTLE? IT'S JUST LIKE WE LEARNED IN THE EDUCORE--
PRIMITIVE MAN, PRONE TO HOSTILITY-- PRISONERS OF THEIR LIMITED BIOLOGY.
DOESN'T MATTER, WIDOW. YOU CAN'T FIGHT THE FUTURE, ESPECIALLY NOT RELICS LIKE THESE.
VAPE 'EM.
FSSS
FSSS

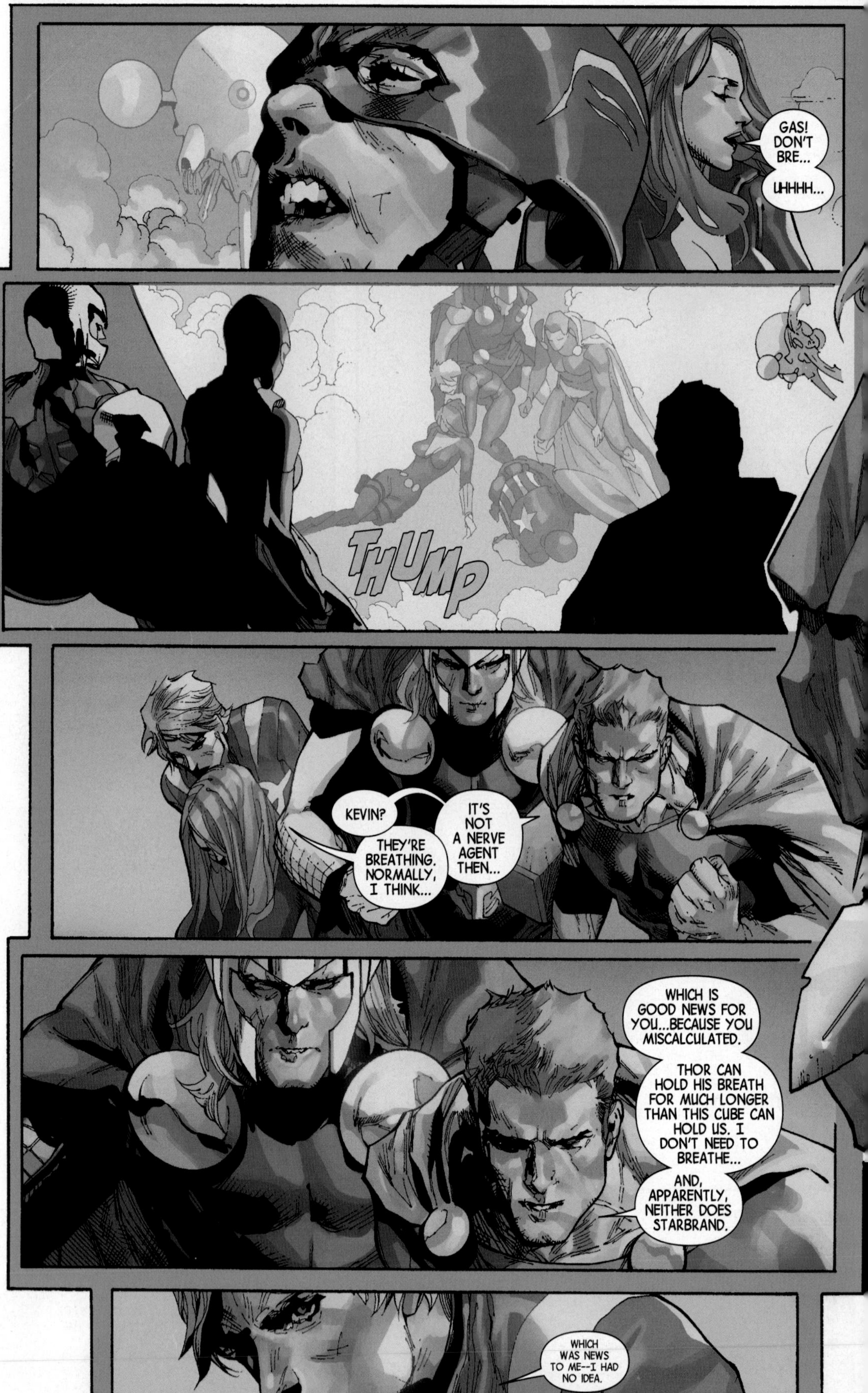
GAS! DON'T BRE...
UHHHH...
THUMP
KEVIN?
THEY'RE BREATHING. NORMALLY, I THINK...
IT'S NOT A NERVE AGENT THEN...
WHICH IS GOOD NEWS FOR YOU...BECAUSE YOU MISCALCULATED.
THOR CAN HOLD HIS BREATH FOR MUCH LONGER THAN THIS CUBE CAN HOLD US. I DON'T NEED TO BREATHE...
AND, APPARENTLY, NEITHER DOES STARBRAND.
WHICH WAS NEWS TO ME--I HAD NO IDEA.

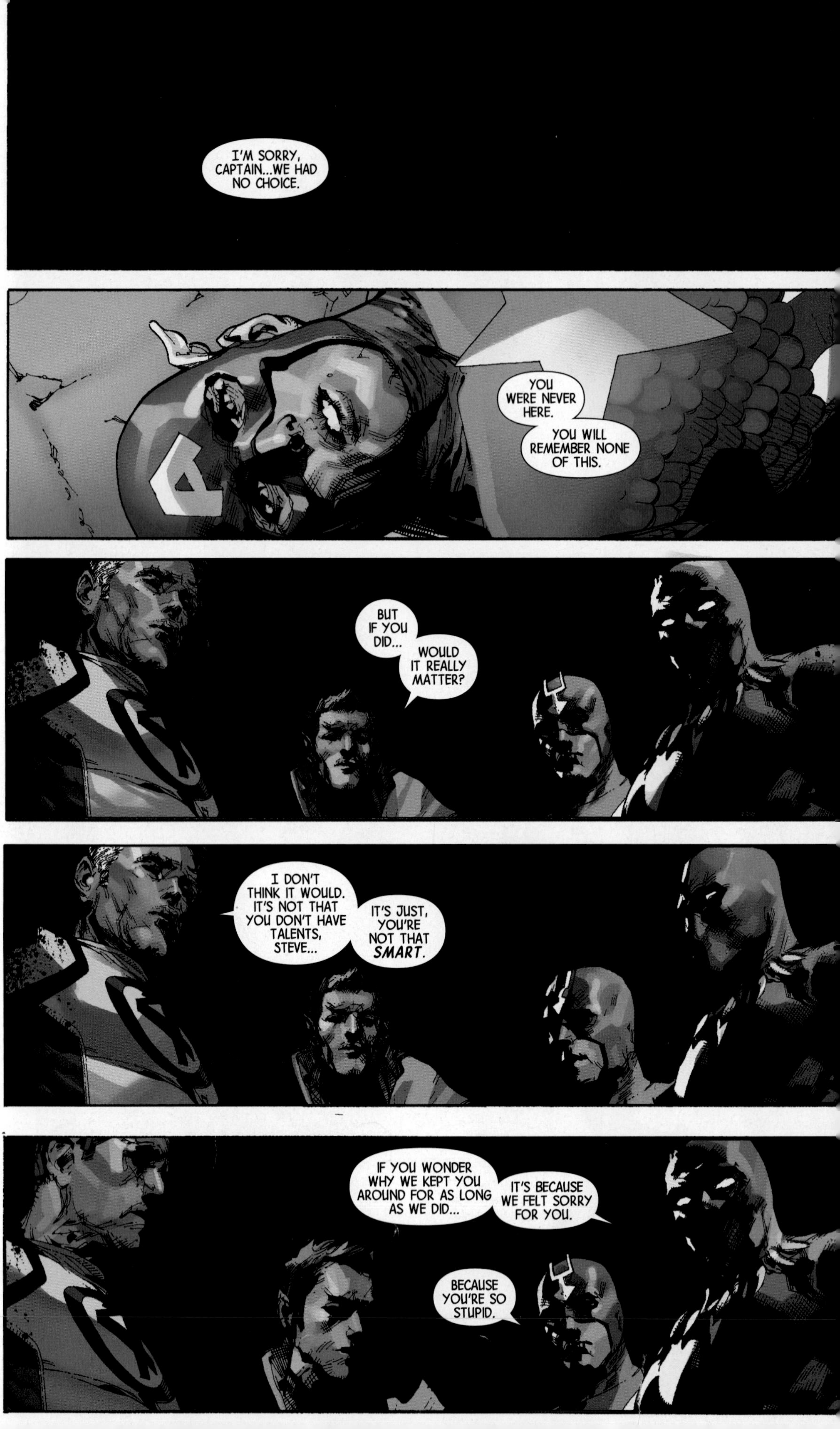
I'M SORRY, CAPTAIN...WE HAD NO CHOICE.
YOU WERE NEVER HERE.
YOU WILL REMEMBER NONE OF THIS.
BUT IF YOU DID...
WOULD IT REALLY MATTER?
I DON'T THINK IT WOULD. IT'S NOT THAT YOU DON'T HAVE TALENTS, STEVE...
IT'S JUST, YOU'RE NOT THAT *SMART*.
IF YOU WONDER WHY WE KEPT YOU AROUND FOR AS LONG AS WE DID...
IT'S BECAUSE WE FELT SORRY FOR YOU.
BECAUSE YOU'RE SO STUPID.

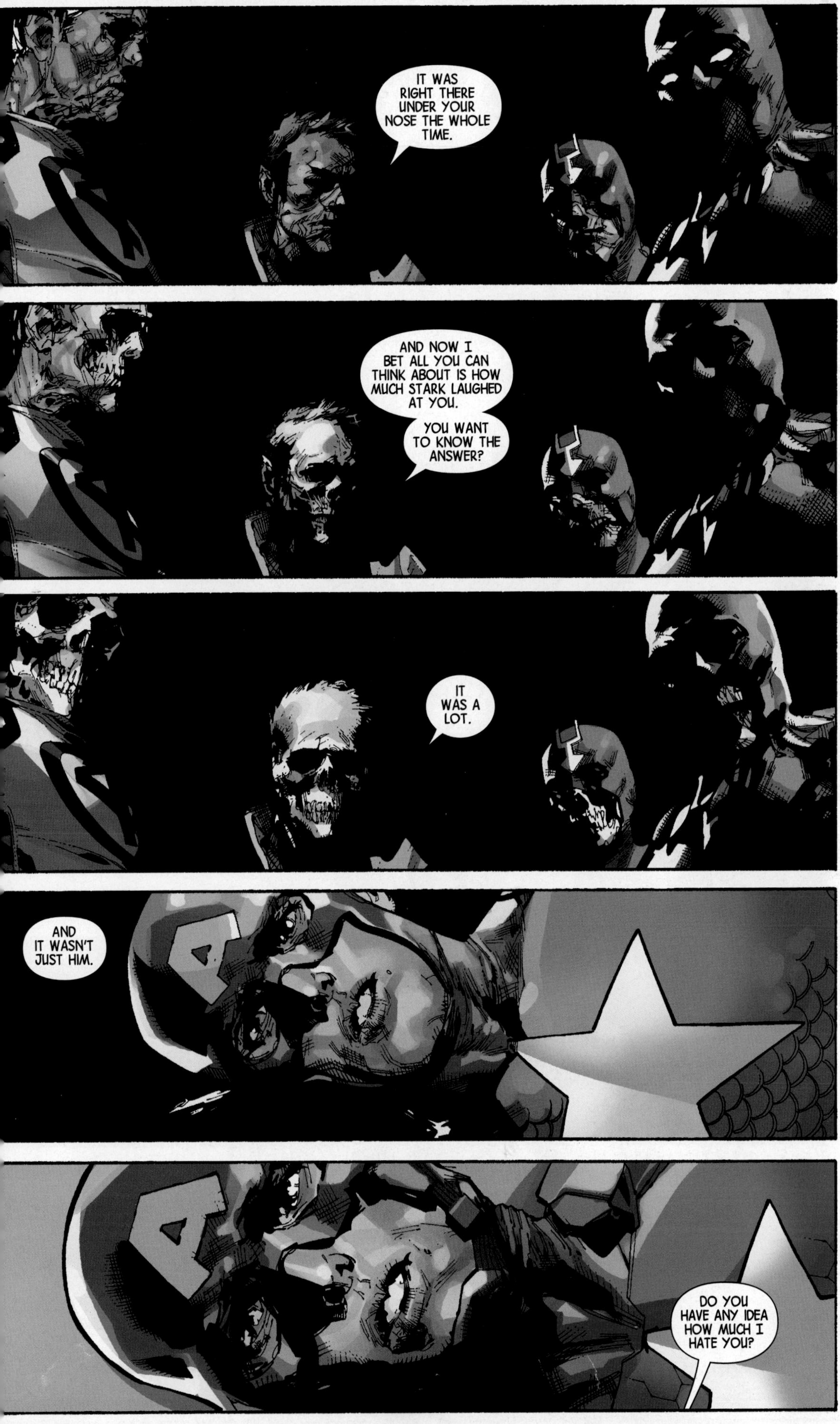
IT WAS RIGHT THERE UNDER YOUR NOSE THE WHOLE TIME.
AND NOW I BET ALL YOU CAN THINK ABOUT IS HOW MUCH STARK LAUGHED AT YOU.
YOU WANT TO KNOW THE ANSWER?
IT WAS A LOT.
AND IT WASN'T JUST HIM.
DO YOU HAVE ANY IDEA HOW MUCH I HATE YOU?

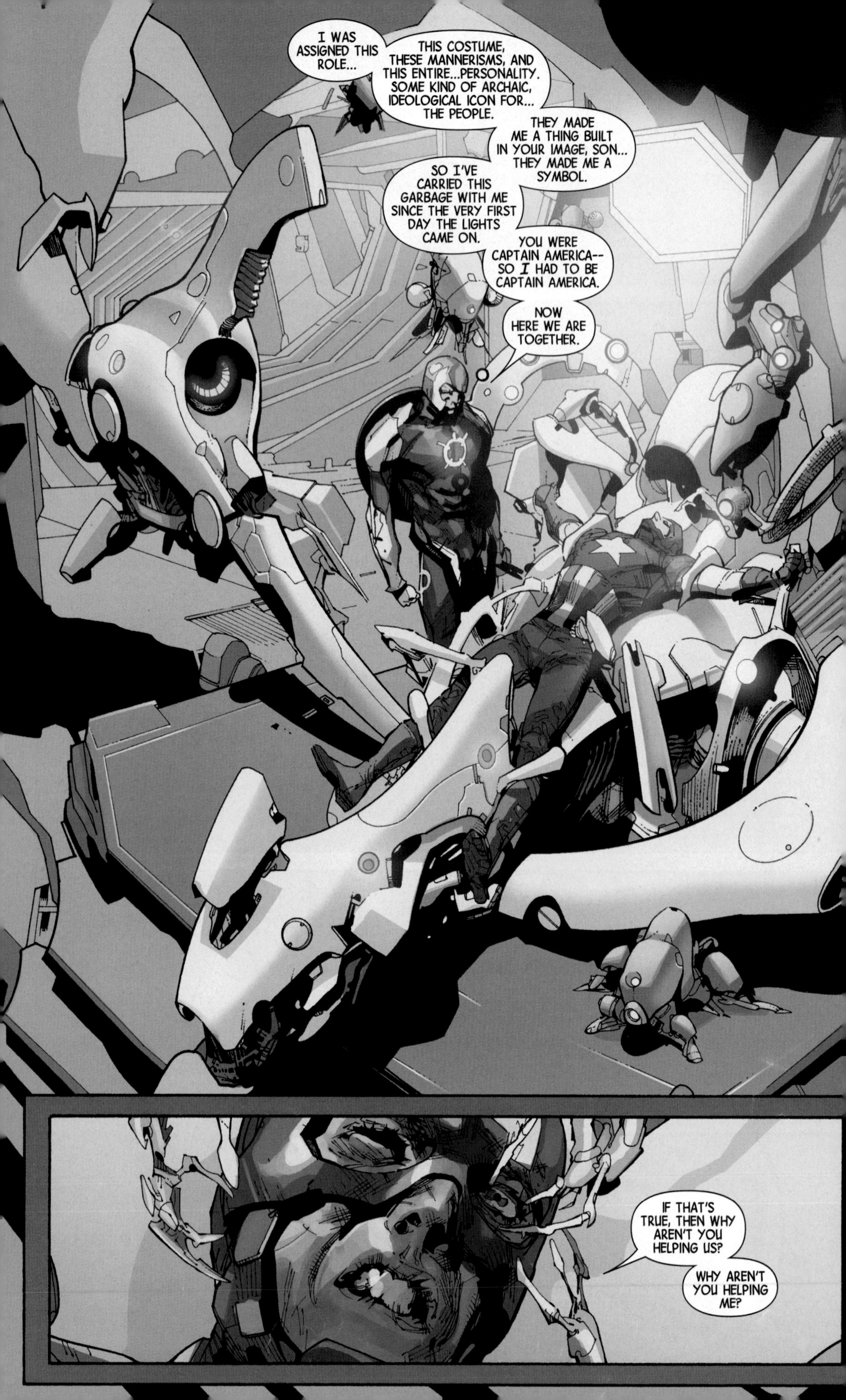
I WAS ASSIGNED THIS ROLE...
THIS COSTUME, THESE MANNERISMS, AND THIS ENTIRE...PERSONALITY. SOME KIND OF ARCHAIC, IDEOLOGICAL ICON FOR... THE PEOPLE.
THEY MADE ME A THING BUILT IN YOUR IMAGE, SON... THEY MADE ME A SYMBOL.
SO I'VE CARRIED THIS GARBAGE WITH ME SINCE THE VERY FIRST DAY THE LIGHTS CAME ON.
YOU WERE CAPTAIN AMERICA-- SO *I* HAD TO BE CAPTAIN AMERICA.
NOW HERE WE ARE TOGETHER.
IF THAT'S TRUE, THEN WHY AREN'T YOU HELPING US?
WHY AREN'T YOU HELPING ME?

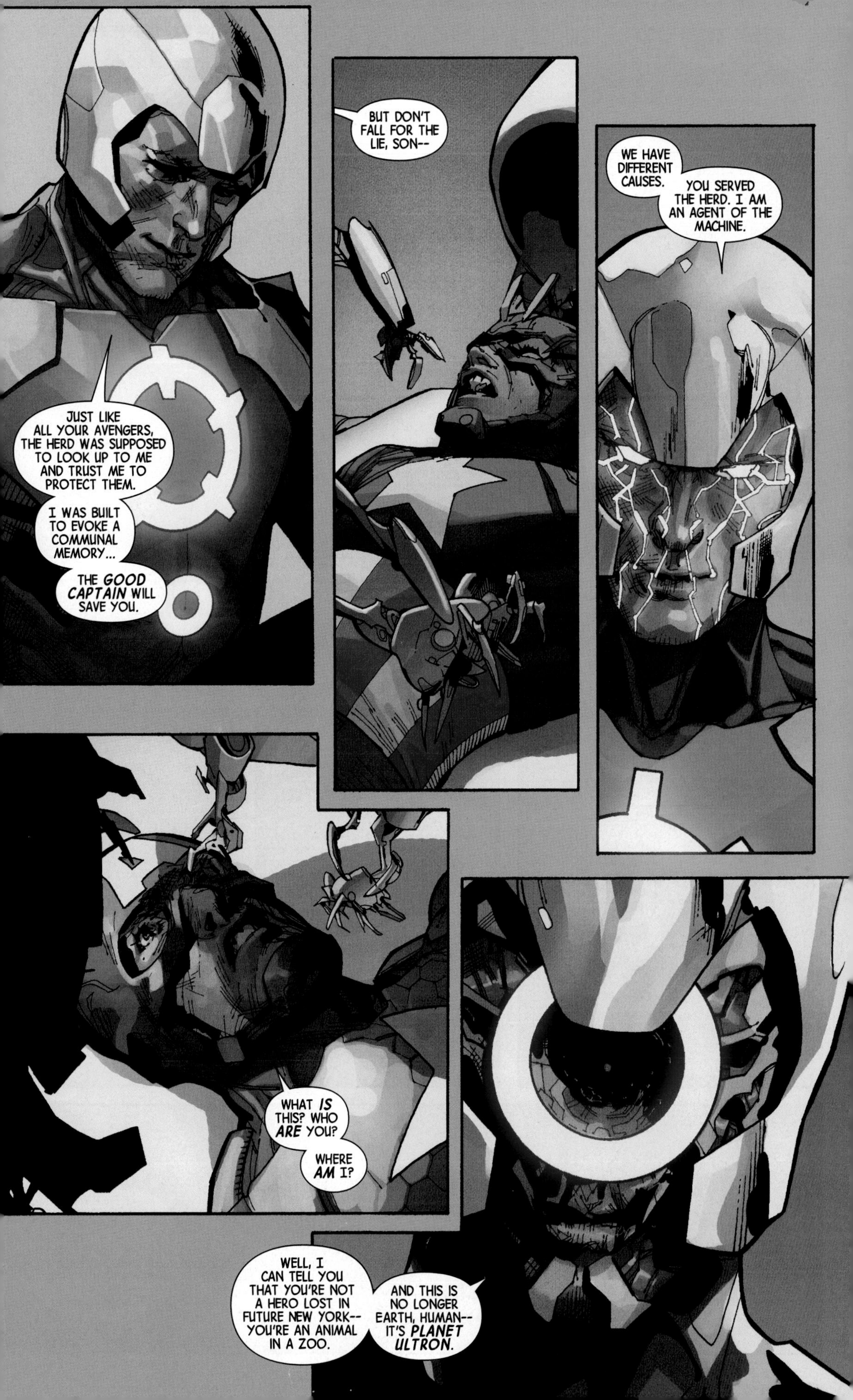
JUST LIKE ALL YOUR AVENGERS, THE HERD WAS SUPPOSED TO LOOK UP TO ME AND TRUST ME TO PROTECT THEM.
I WAS BUILT TO EVOKE A COMMUNAL MEMORY...
THE *GOOD CAPTAIN* WILL SAVE YOU.
BUT DON'T FALL FOR THE LIE, SON--
WE HAVE DIFFERENT CAUSES.
YOU SERVED THE HERD. I AM AN AGENT OF THE MACHINE.
WHAT *IS* THIS? WHO *ARE* YOU?
WHERE *AM* I?
WELL, I CAN TELL YOU THAT YOU'RE NOT A HERO LOST IN FUTURE NEW YORK-- YOU'RE AN ANIMAL IN A ZOO.
AND THIS IS NO LONGER EARTH, HUMAN-- IT'S *PLANET ULTRON*.

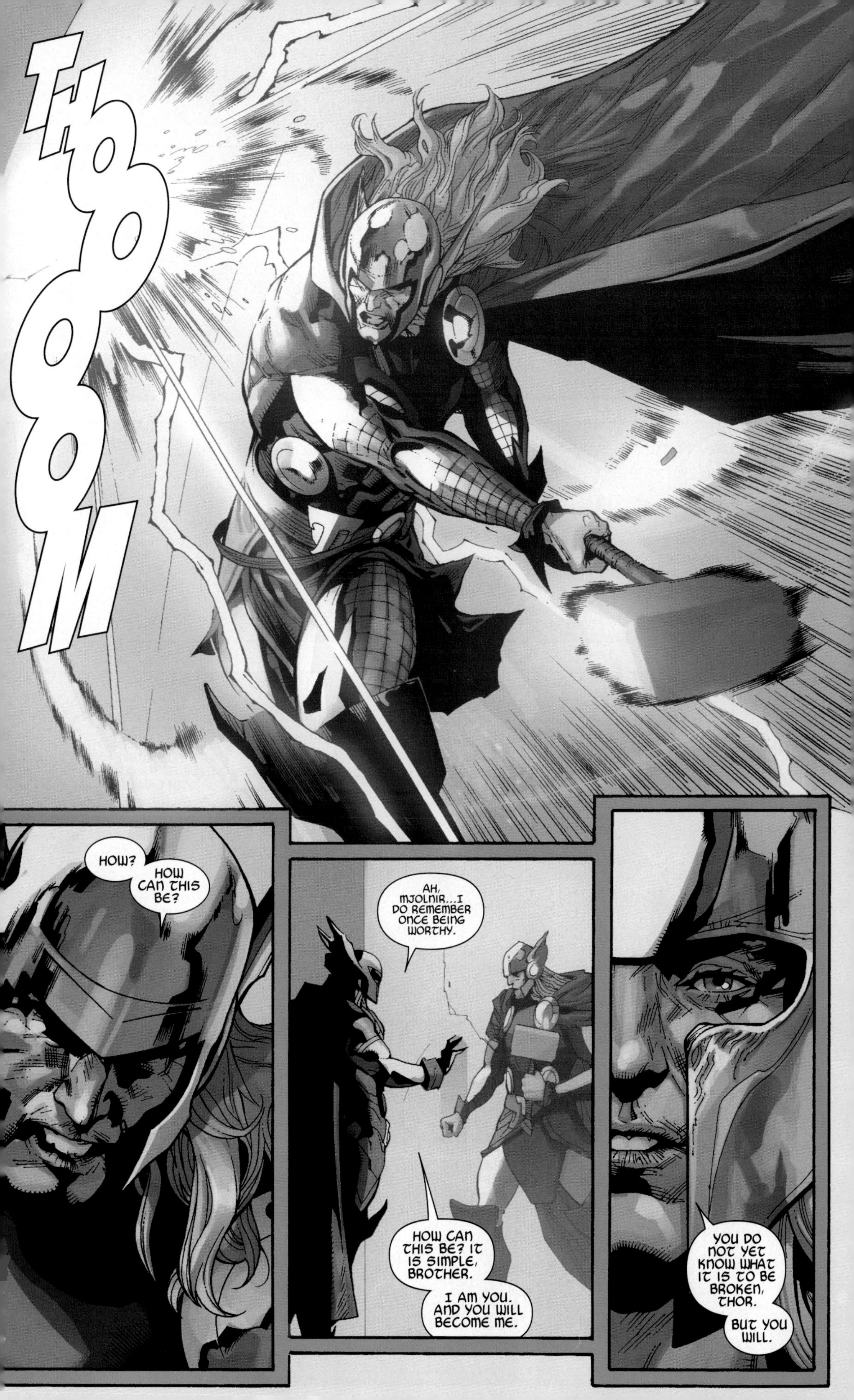
THOOOOOOM
HOW?
HOW CAN THIS BE?
AH, MJOLNIR...I DO REMEMBER ONCE BEING WORTHY.
HOW CAN THIS BE? IT IS SIMPLE, BROTHER.
I AM YOU. AND YOU WILL BECOME ME.
YOU DO NOT YET KNOW WHAT IT IS TO BE BROKEN, THOR.
BUT YOU WILL.

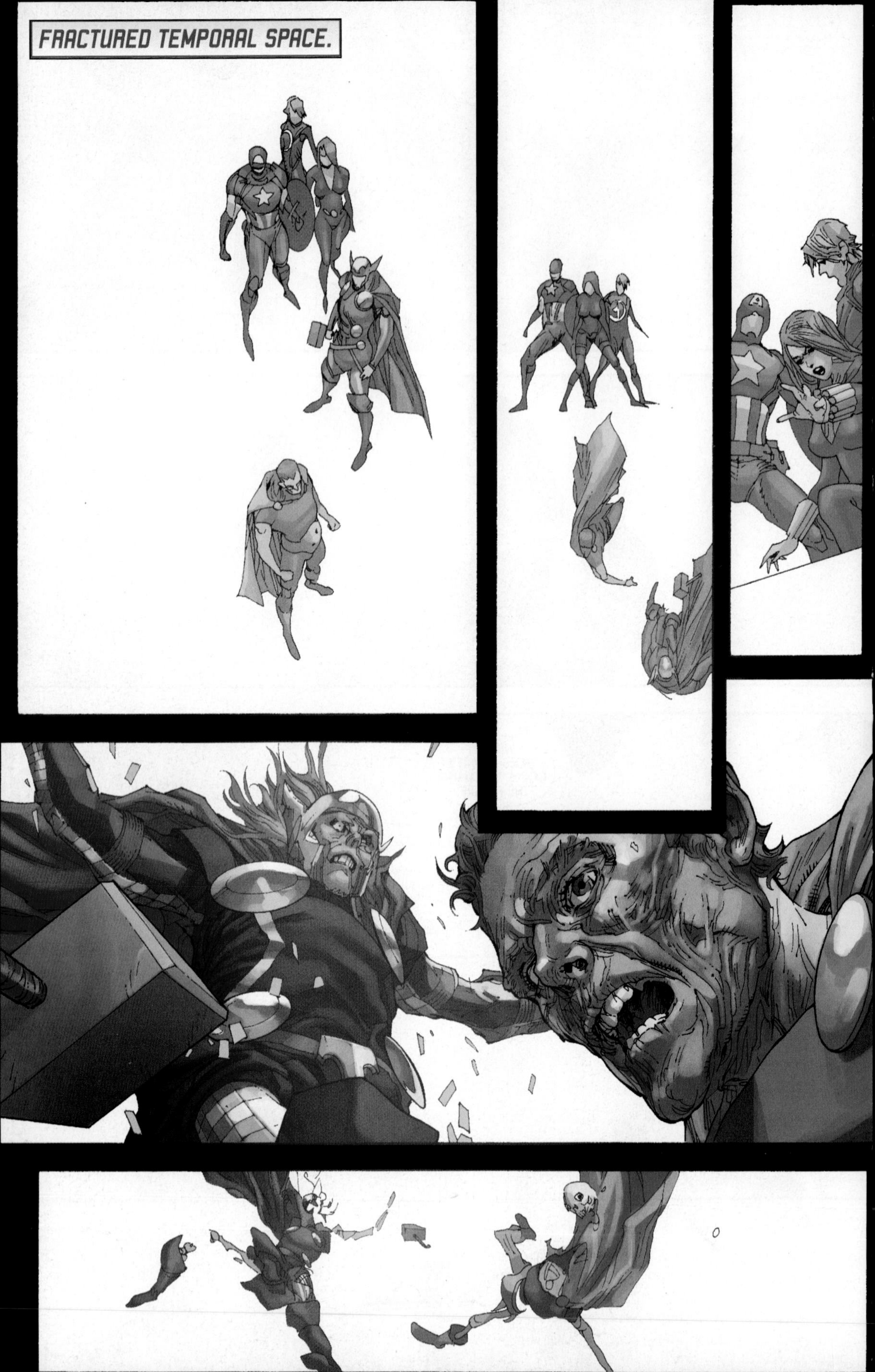
FRACTURED TEMPORAL SPACE.

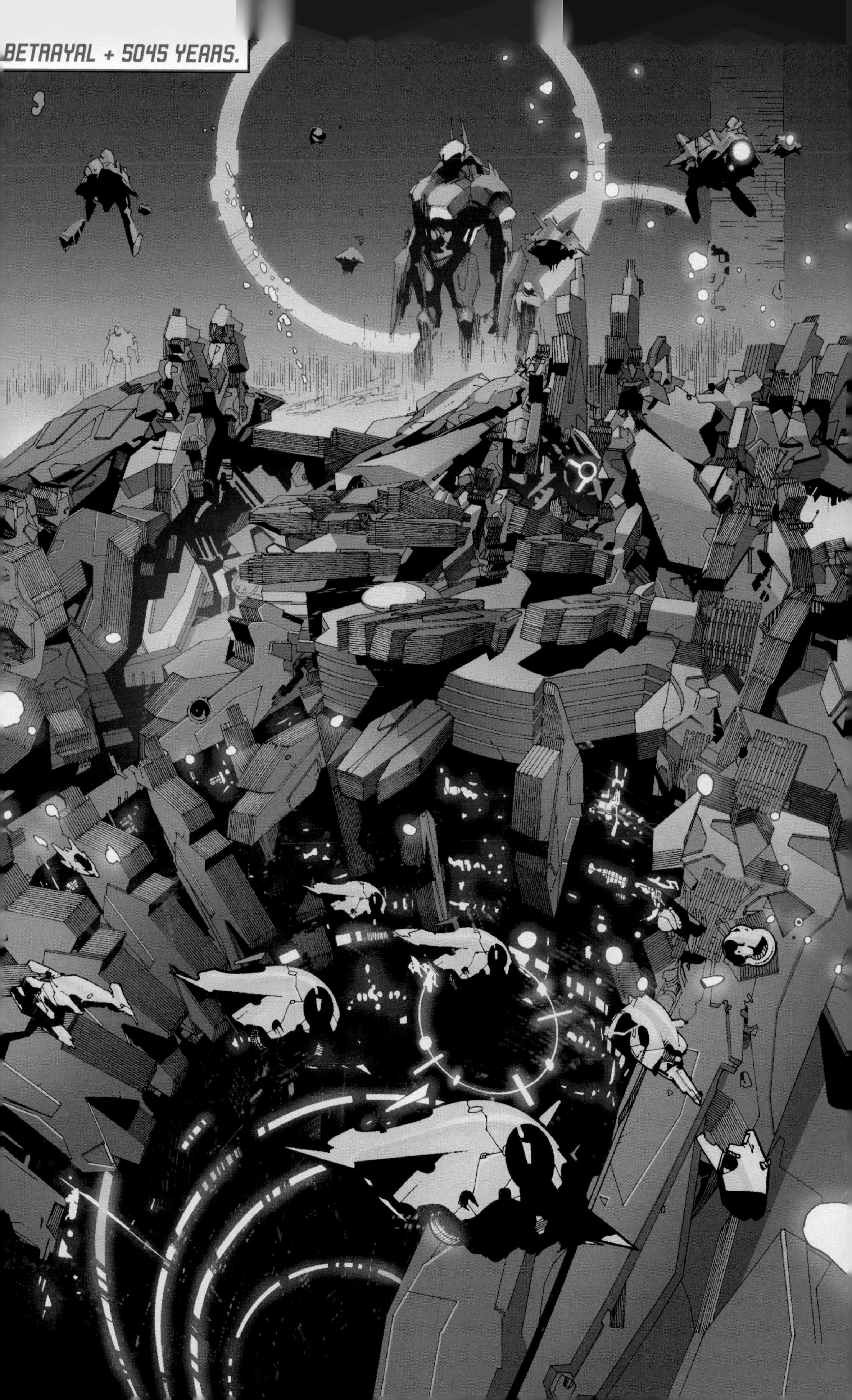
BETRAYAL + 5045 YEARS.

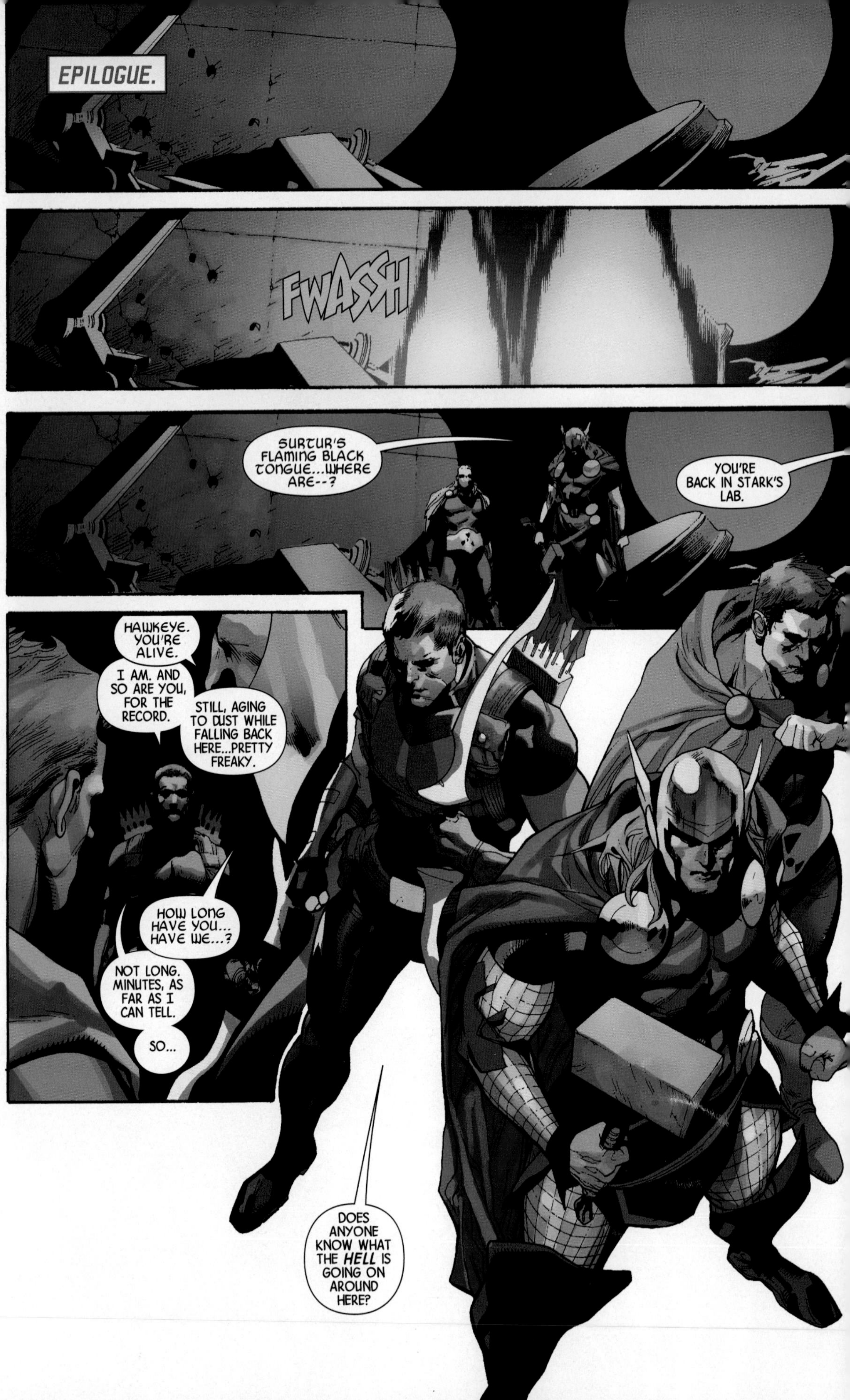
EPILOGUE.
FWASSH
SURTUR'S FLAMING BLACK TONGUE...WHERE ARE--?
YOU'RE BACK IN STARK'S LAB.
HAWKEYE. YOU'RE ALIVE.
I AM. AND SO ARE YOU, FOR THE RECORD.
STILL, AGING TO DUST WHILE FALLING BACK HERE...PRETTY FREAKY.
HOW LONG HAVE YOU... HAVE WE...?
NOT LONG. MINUTES, AS FAR AS I CAN TELL.
SO...
DOES ANYONE KNOW WHAT THE HELL IS GOING ON AROUND HERE?

"FIVE THOUSAND INTO THE FUTURE"

FWASH

LONG GROWTH VEGETATION. THIS TREE IS MASSIVE... HUNDREDS OF YEARS OLD.

THIS IS NOT WHAT I WAS EXPECTING.

YEAH. NOT A FAN OF SCIENCE FICTION, BUT IS THIS AN H.G. WELLS THING?

OR DID WE TRAVEL **BACKWARDS** IN TIME?

IT'S A TRICK.

WELL, NOT A TRICK...IT'S REAL, BUT THIS IS DEFINITELY AN ADVANCED SOCIETY--MILLIONS OF PEOPLE LIVING ON THE MOON AND A VERY TALKATIVE GLOBAL A.I. RUNNING THE MEGACITIES HERE ON EARTH.

SO IT'S A GARDEN?

OH, YOU'LL FIND IT'S MUCH MORE THAN THAT...

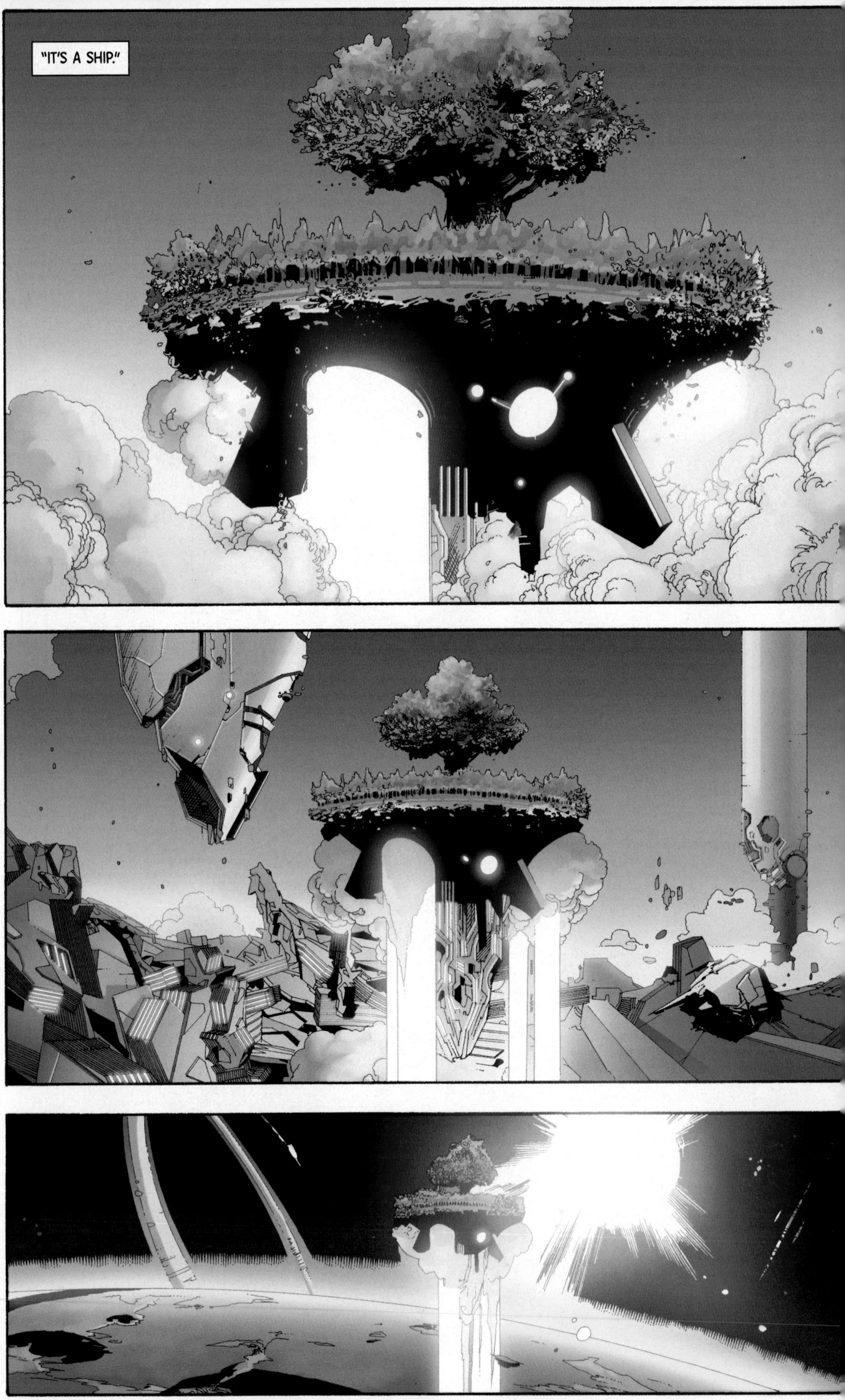
"IT'S A SHIP."

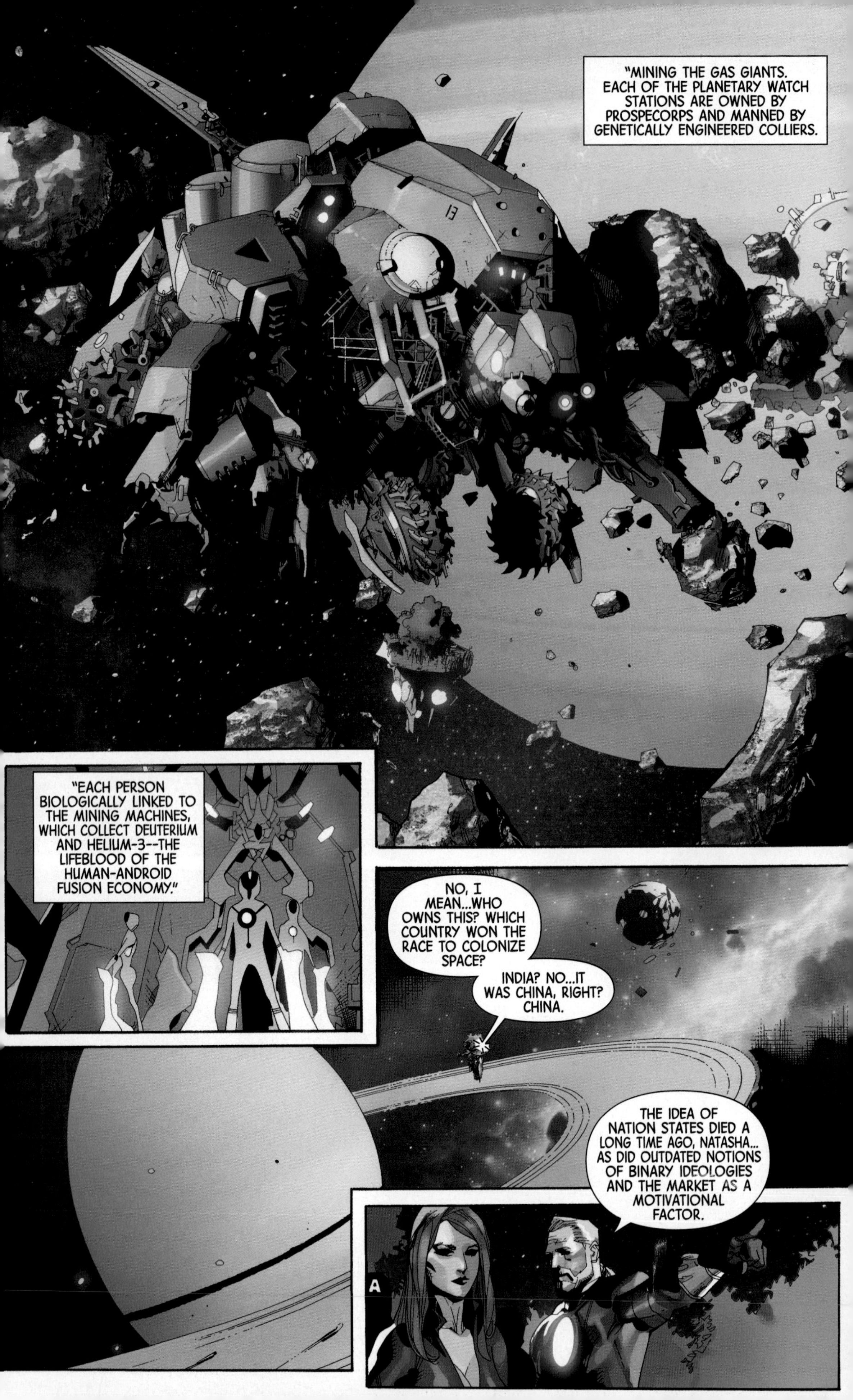
"MINING THE GAS GIANTS. EACH OF THE PLANETARY WATCH STATIONS ARE OWNED BY PROSPECORPS AND MANNED BY GENETICALLY ENGINEERED COLLIERS.
"EACH PERSON BIOLOGICALLY LINKED TO THE MINING MACHINES, WHICH COLLECT DEUTERIUM AND HELIUM-3--THE LIFEBLOOD OF THE HUMAN-ANDROID FUSION ECONOMY."
NO, I MEAN...WHO OWNS THIS? WHICH COUNTRY WON THE RACE TO COLONIZE SPACE?
INDIA? NO...IT WAS CHINA, RIGHT? CHINA.
THE IDEA OF NATION STATES DIED A LONG TIME AGO, NATASHA... AS DID OUTDATED NOTIONS OF BINARY IDEOLOGIES AND THE MARKET AS A MOTIVATIONAL FACTOR.
A

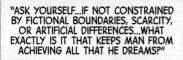

"ASK YOURSELF...IF NOT CONSTRAINED BY FICTIONAL BOUNDARIES, SCARCITY, OR ARTIFICIAL DIFFERENCES...WHAT EXACTLY IS IT THAT KEEPS MAN FROM ACHIEVING ALL THAT HE DREAMS?"

NOTHING.

IN THIS TIME, MORE PEOPLE LIVE IN THE OUTER COLONIES OF OUR SOLAR SYSTEM THAN EARTH ITSELF. ALMOST 30 BILLION.

SO, NOW... SPACE, AND SOON, *BEYOND THAT.*

HEY, SORRY TO INTERRUPT... BUT IS ANY OF THIS EDIBLE? I'M STARVING.

ASSUMING WE'RE NO LONGER CONSTRAINED BY SCARCITY AND ALL THAT... OH, AND THIS FUTURE SPACE FRUIT IS OKAY TO EAT OR WHATEVER...

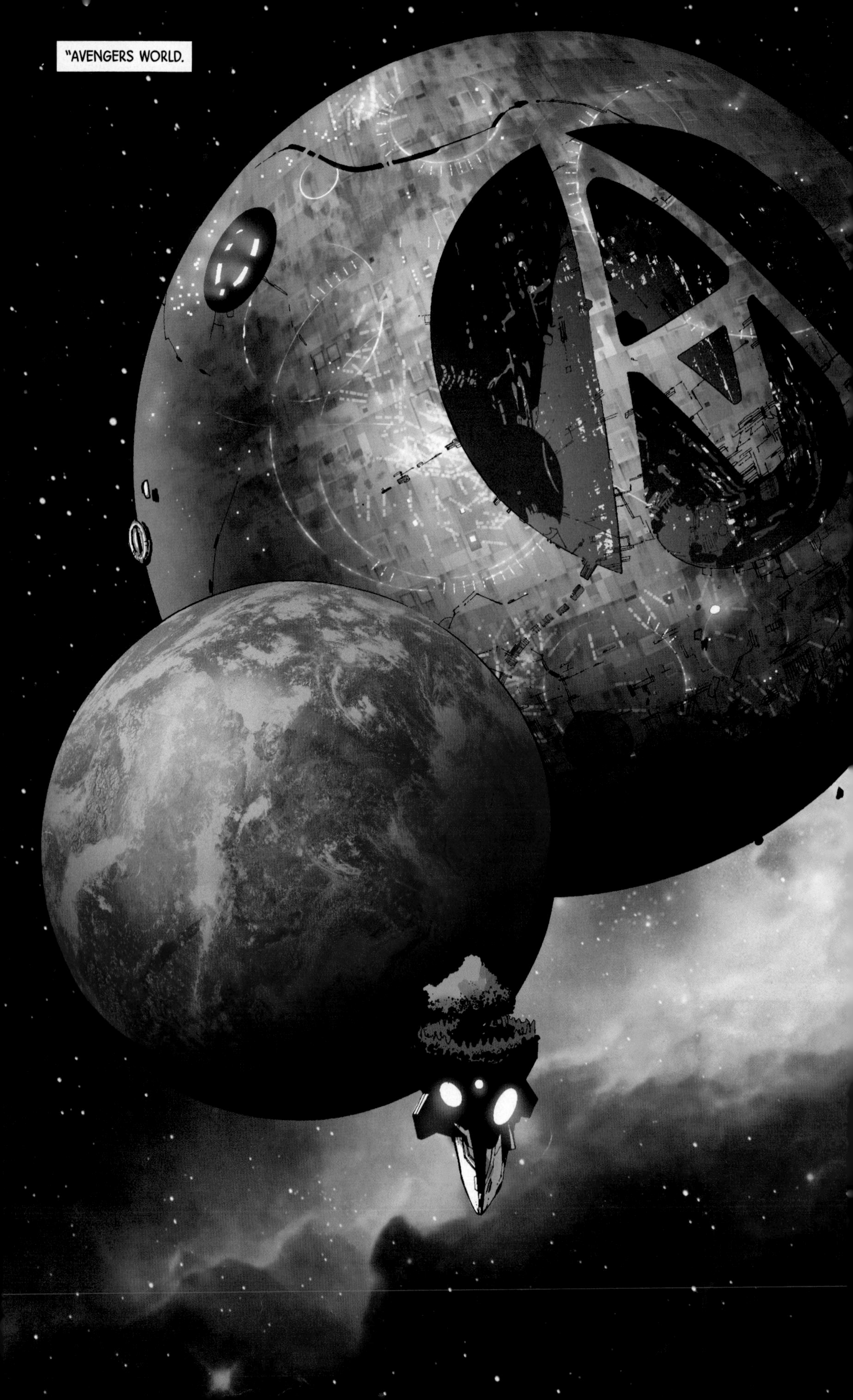
"AVENGERS WORLD.

"THE UTOPIAN SUPERPLANET IS HUB-HOME TO BILLIONS OF UNIVERSAL SUPERBEINGS. FROM *THIS WORLD*, THE AVENGERS UNIVERSE IS KEPT HYPERDYNAMICALLY STABLE BY ITS GUARDIANS.

"THE REMNANTS OF YOUR AVENGERS MACHINE--ALIGNED WITH THE IMPERIAL ACADEMY, THE UNITED UNIVERSAL HOUSES OF THE INHUMANS, AND THE ATEMPORAL ARCHITECTS OF S.H.I.E.L.D.--CAST A WIDE NET FROM AVENGERS WORLD...

"PROTECTING AND POLICING THE KNOWN UNIVERSES.

"LOOK! EVEN NOW, THE WORLD'S MECHATYPES HAVE CAPTURED A ROGUE PLANET AND ARE PREPARING TO HURL IT BACKWARDS THROUGH SPACE AND TIME TO FULFILL THE FRONTEND OF A CLOSED-ACTION LOOP."

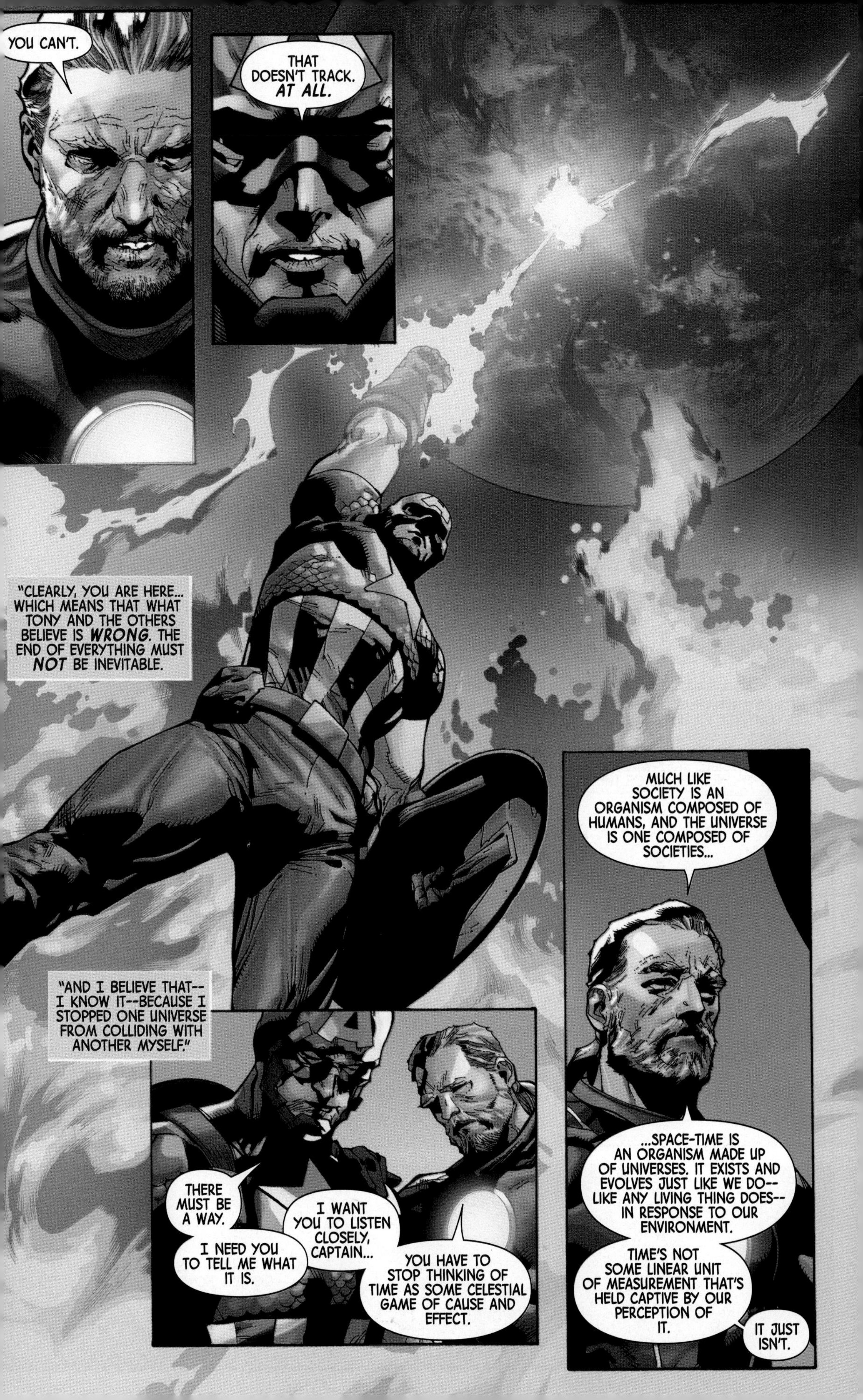

YOU CAN'T.
THAT DOESN'T TRACK. AT ALL.
"CLEARLY, YOU ARE HERE... WHICH MEANS THAT WHAT TONY AND THE OTHERS BELIEVE IS WRONG. THE END OF EVERYTHING MUST NOT BE INEVITABLE.
"AND I BELIEVE THAT-- I KNOW IT--BECAUSE I STOPPED ONE UNIVERSE FROM COLLIDING WITH ANOTHER MYSELF."
THERE MUST BE A WAY.
I NEED YOU TO TELL ME WHAT IT IS.
I WANT YOU TO LISTEN CLOSELY, CAPTAIN...
YOU HAVE TO STOP THINKING OF TIME AS SOME CELESTIAL GAME OF CAUSE AND EFFECT.
MUCH LIKE SOCIETY IS AN ORGANISM COMPOSED OF HUMANS, AND THE UNIVERSE IS ONE COMPOSED OF SOCIETIES...
...SPACE-TIME IS AN ORGANISM MADE UP OF UNIVERSES. IT EXISTS AND EVOLVES JUST LIKE WE DO-- LIKE ANY LIVING THING DOES-- IN RESPONSE TO OUR ENVIRONMENT.
TIME'S NOT SOME LINEAR UNIT OF MEASUREMENT THAT'S HELD CAPTIVE BY OUR PERCEPTION OF IT.
IT JUST ISN'T.

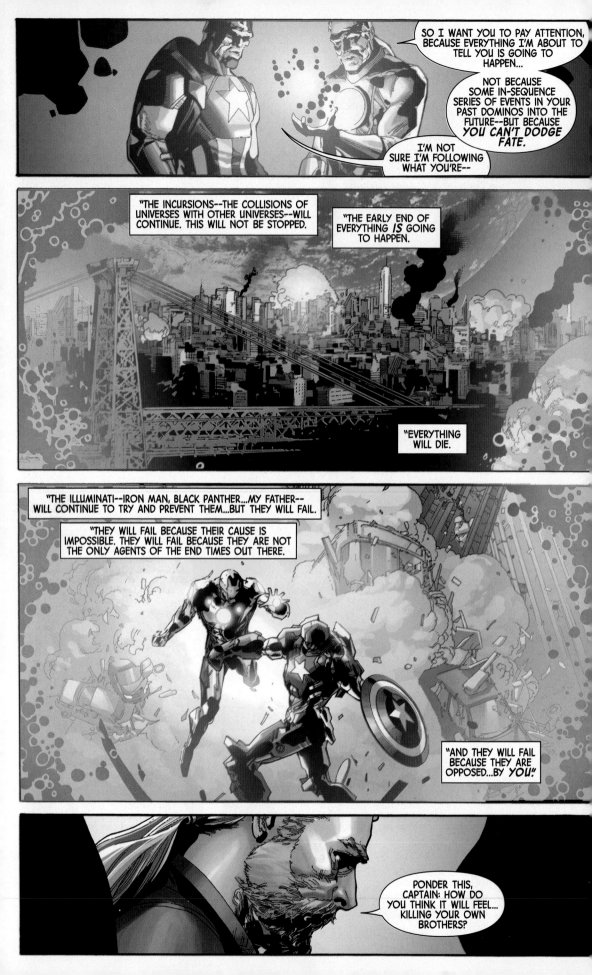

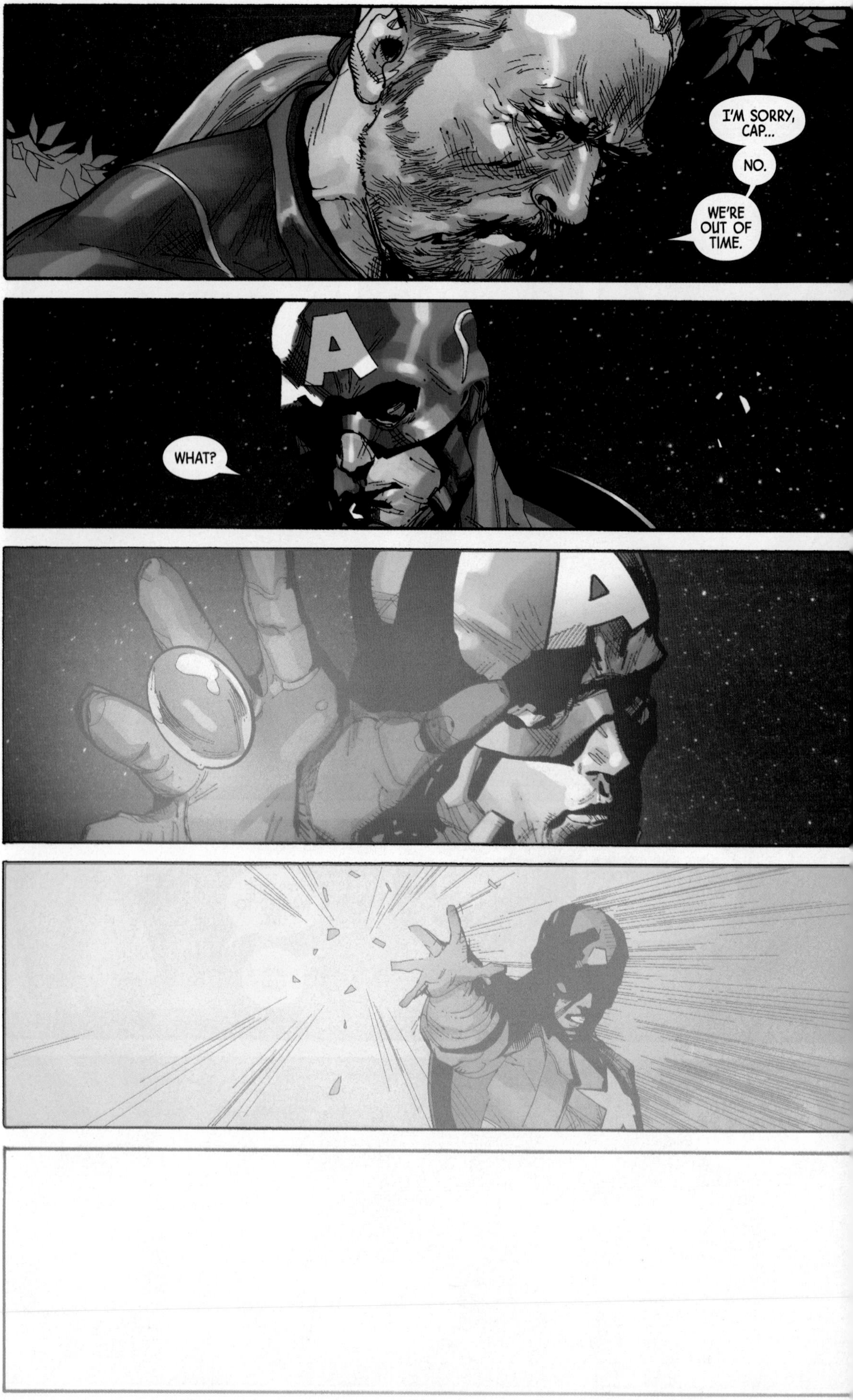
I'M SORRY, CAP...
NO.
WE'RE OUT OF TIME.
WHAT?

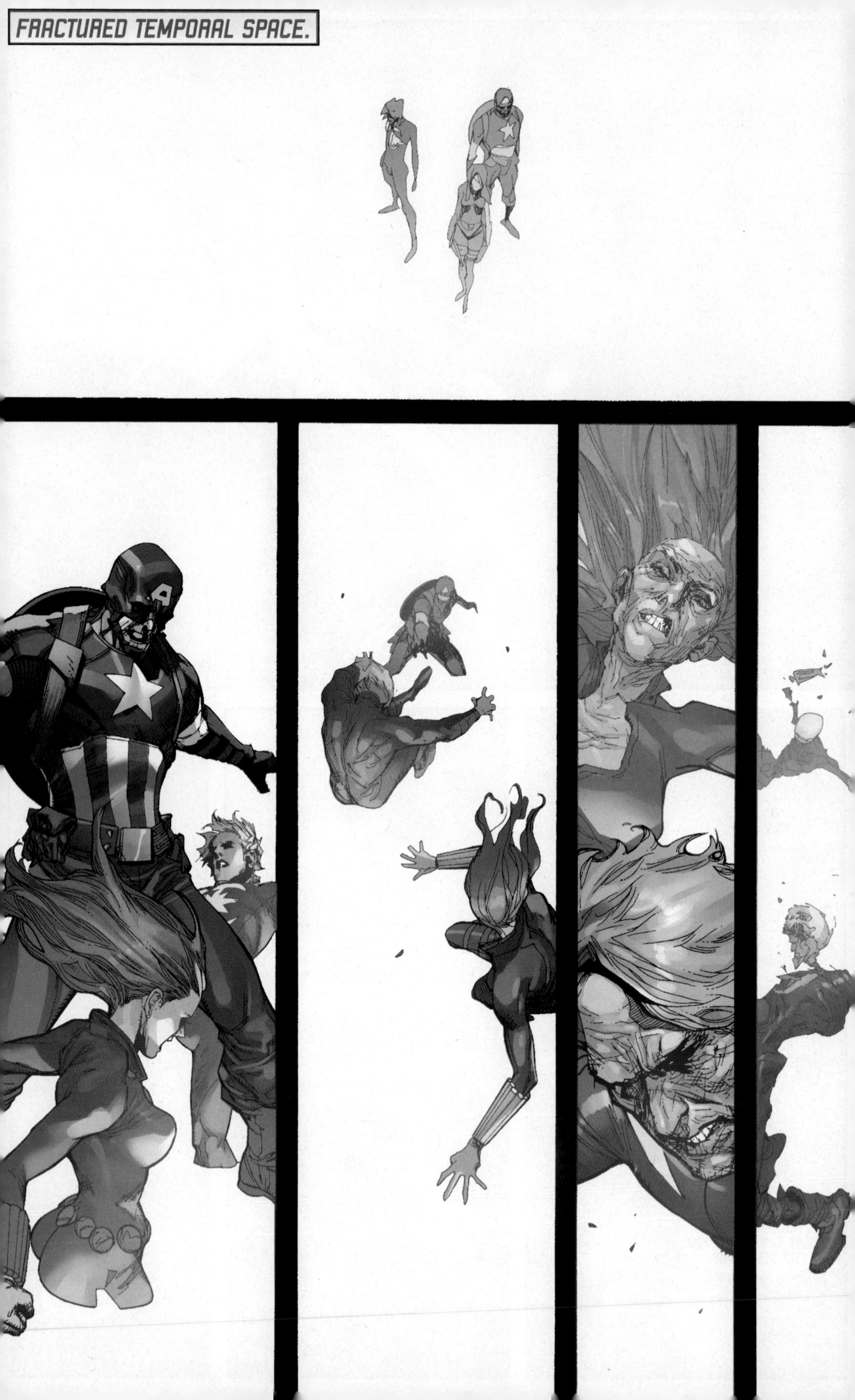
FRACTURED TEMPORAL SPACE.

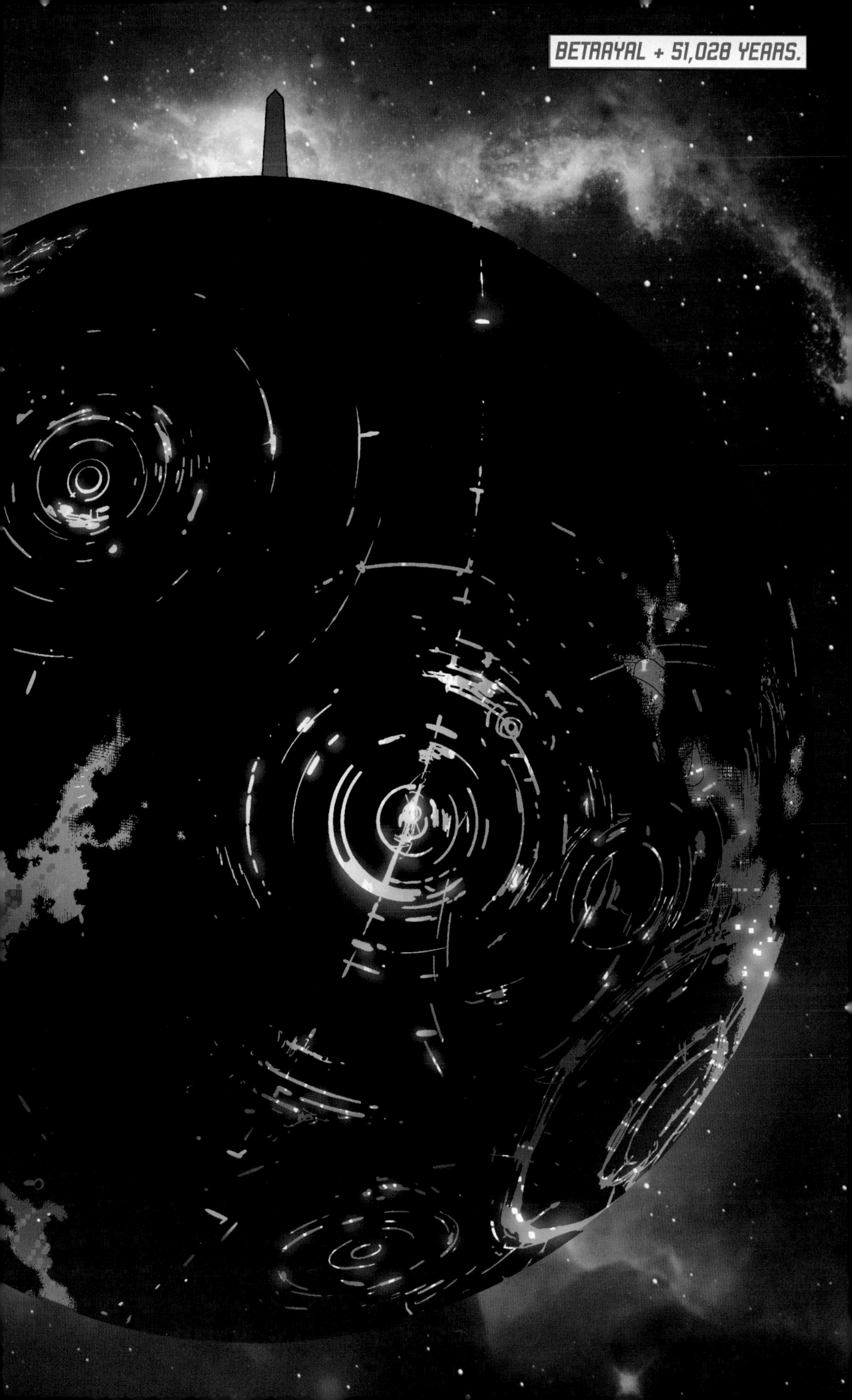
BETRAYAL + 51,028 YEARS.

"FIFTY THOUSAND INTO THE FUTURE"

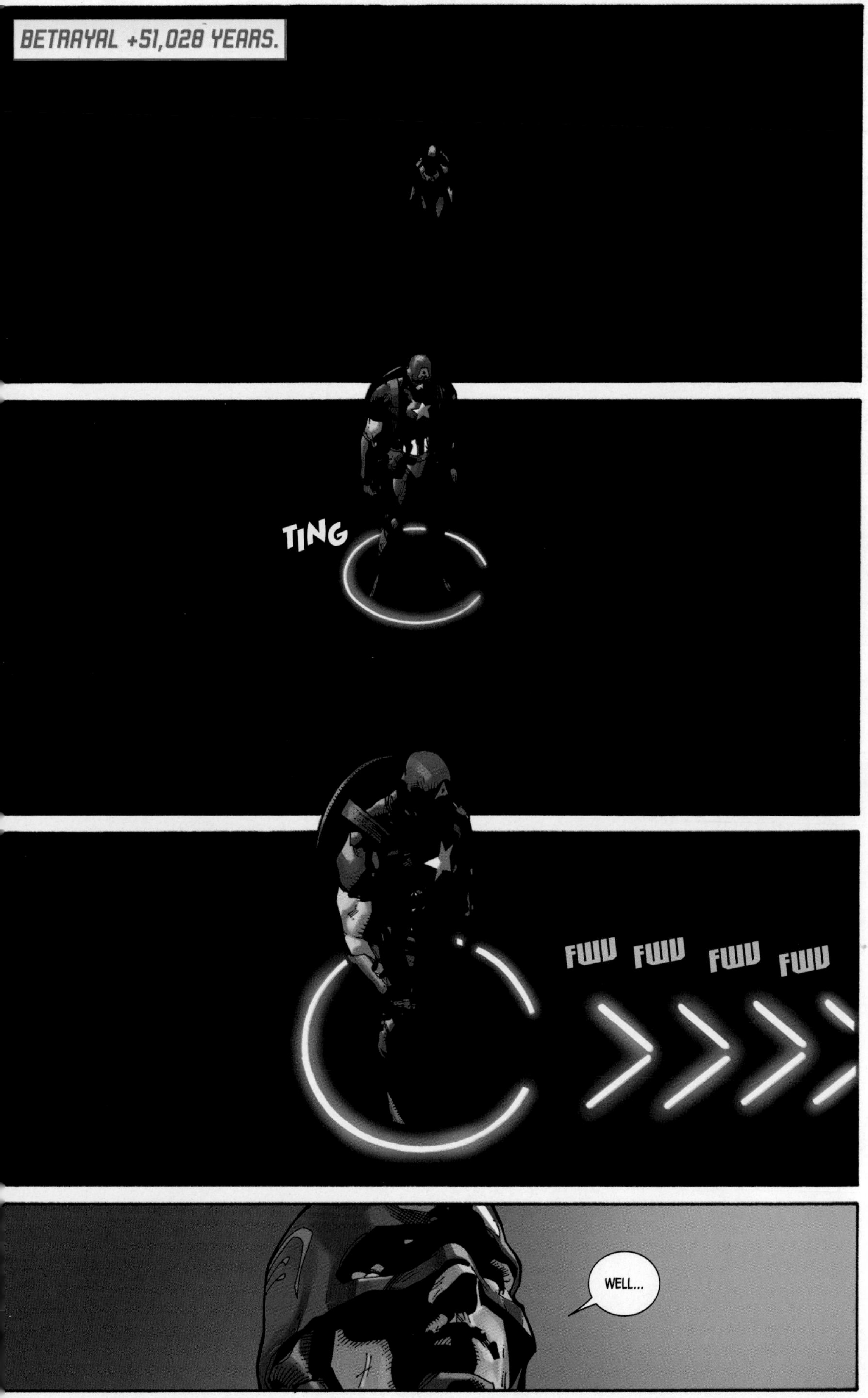
BETRAYAL +51,028 YEARS.
TING
FWV FWV FWV FWV
WELL...

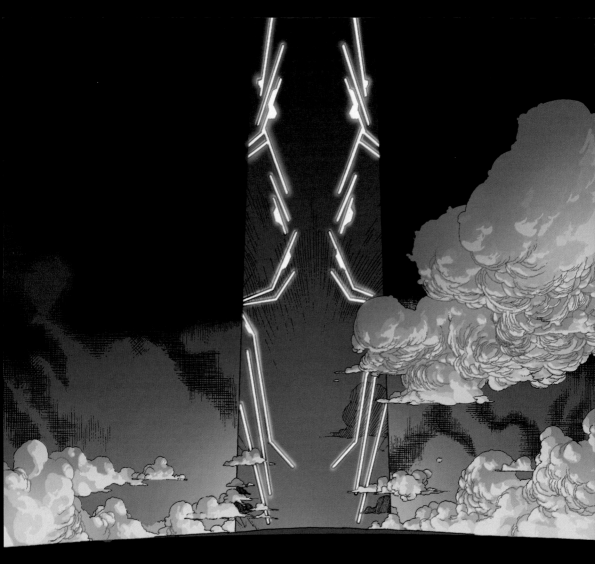

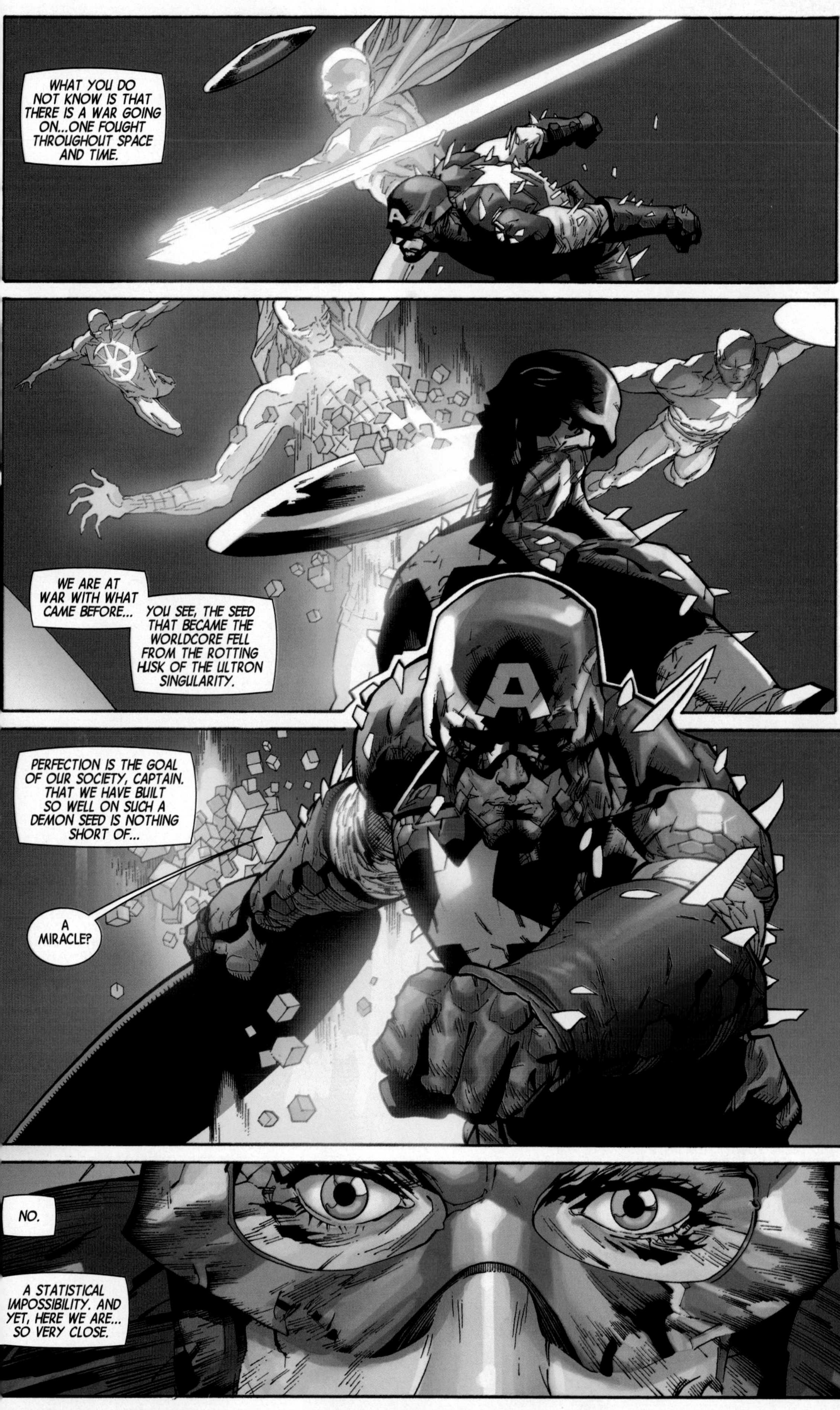
WHAT YOU DO NOT KNOW IS THAT THERE IS A WAR GOING ON...ONE FOUGHT THROUGHOUT SPACE AND TIME.
WE ARE AT WAR WITH WHAT CAME BEFORE...
YOU SEE, THE SEED THAT BECAME THE WORLDCORE FELL FROM THE ROTTING HUSK OF THE ULTRON SINGULARITY.
PERFECTION IS THE GOAL OF OUR SOCIETY, CAPTAIN. THAT WE HAVE BUILT SO WELL ON SUCH A DEMON SEED IS NOTHING SHORT OF...
A MIRACLE?
NO.
A STATISTICAL IMPOSSIBILITY. AND YET, HERE WE ARE... SO VERY CLOSE.

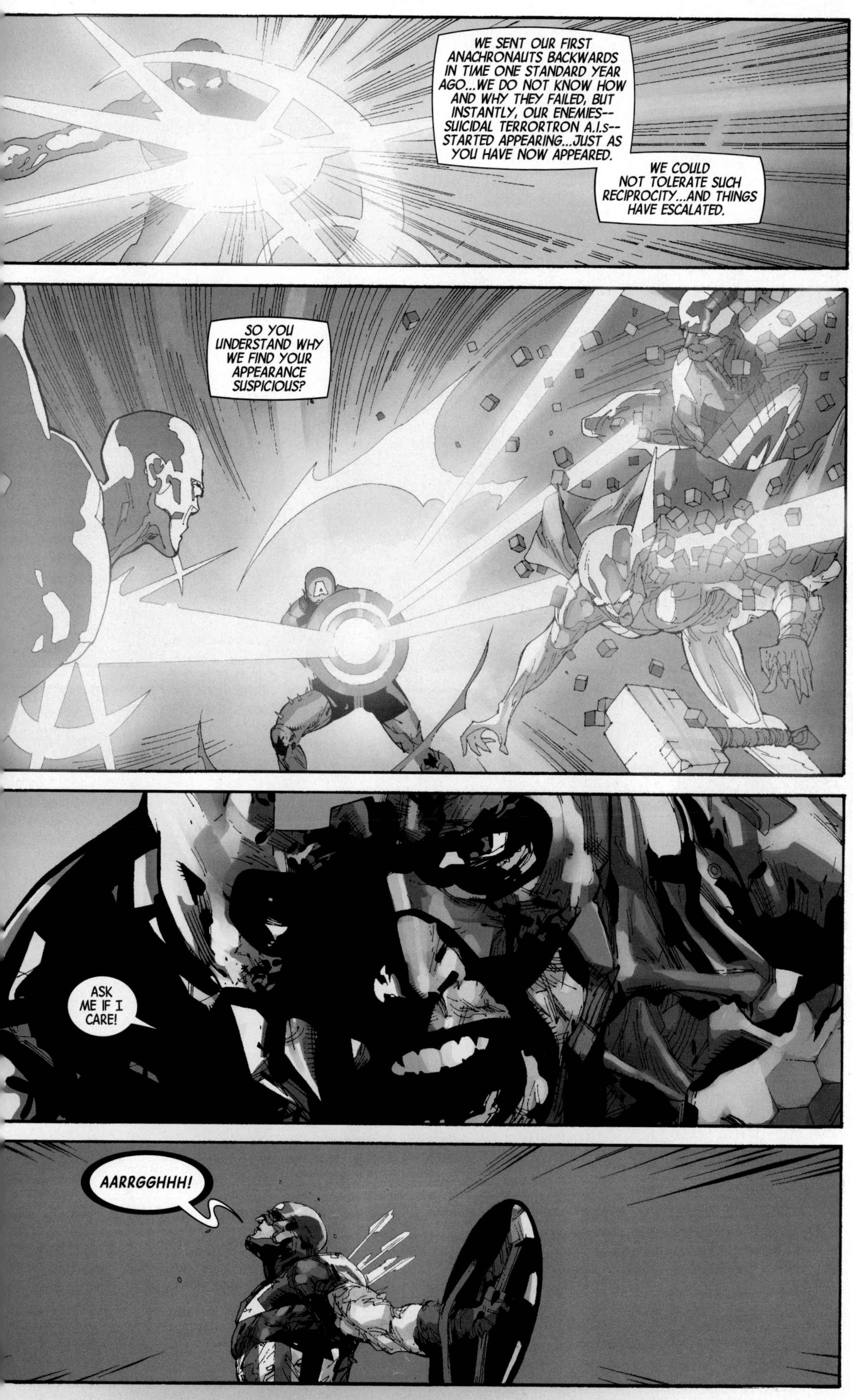
WE SENT OUR FIRST ANACHRONAUTS BACKWARDS IN TIME ONE STANDARD YEAR AGO...WE DO NOT KNOW HOW AND WHY THEY FAILED, BUT INSTANTLY, OUR ENEMIES--SUICIDAL TERRORTRON A.I.s--STARTED APPEARING...JUST AS YOU HAVE NOW APPEARED.
WE COULD NOT TOLERATE SUCH RECIPROCITY...AND THINGS HAVE ESCALATED.
SO YOU UNDERSTAND WHY WE FIND YOUR APPEARANCE SUSPICIOUS?
ASK ME IF I CARE!
AARRGGHHH!

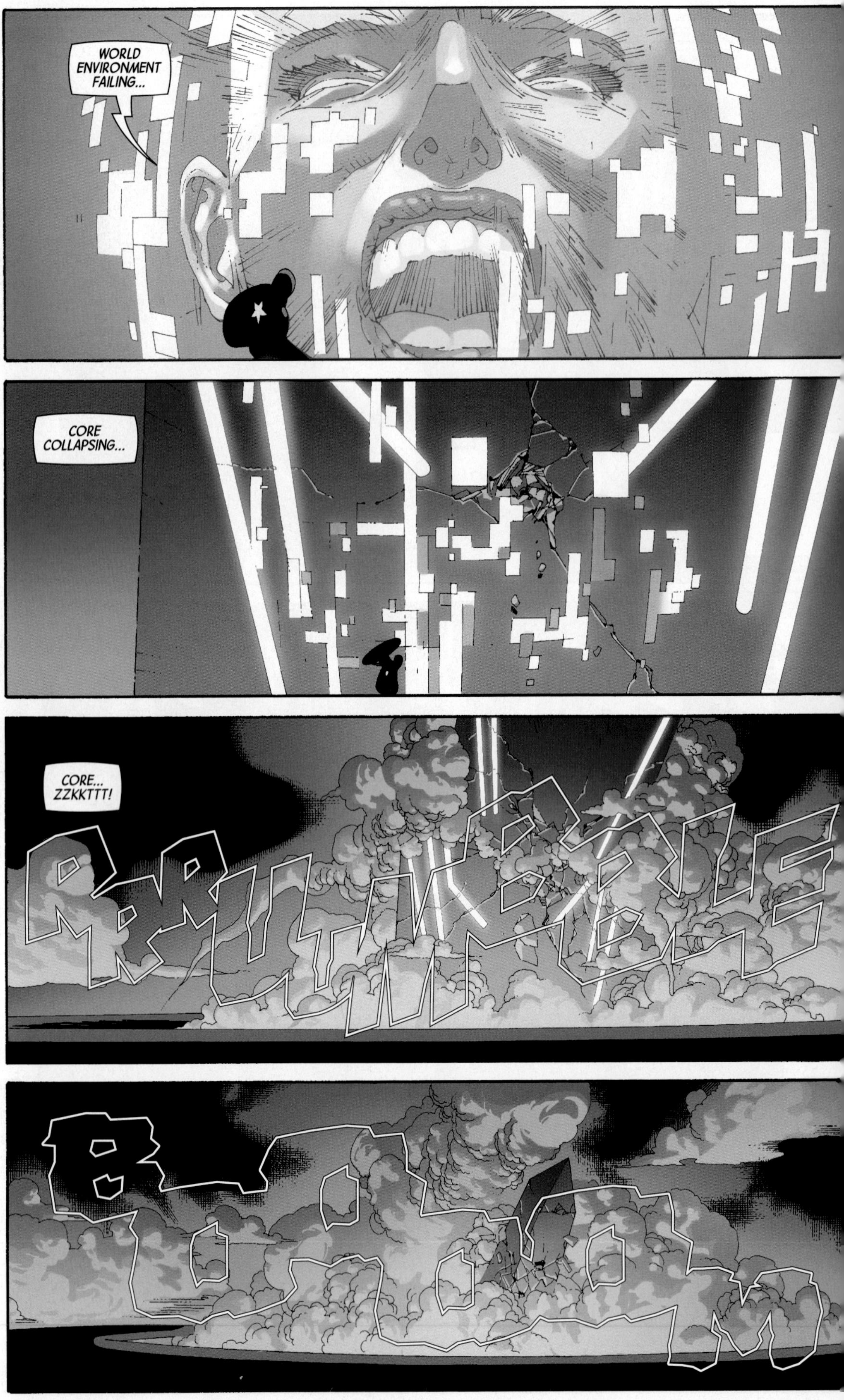
WORLD ENVIRONMENT FAILING...
CORE COLLAPSING...
CORE... ZZKKTTT!

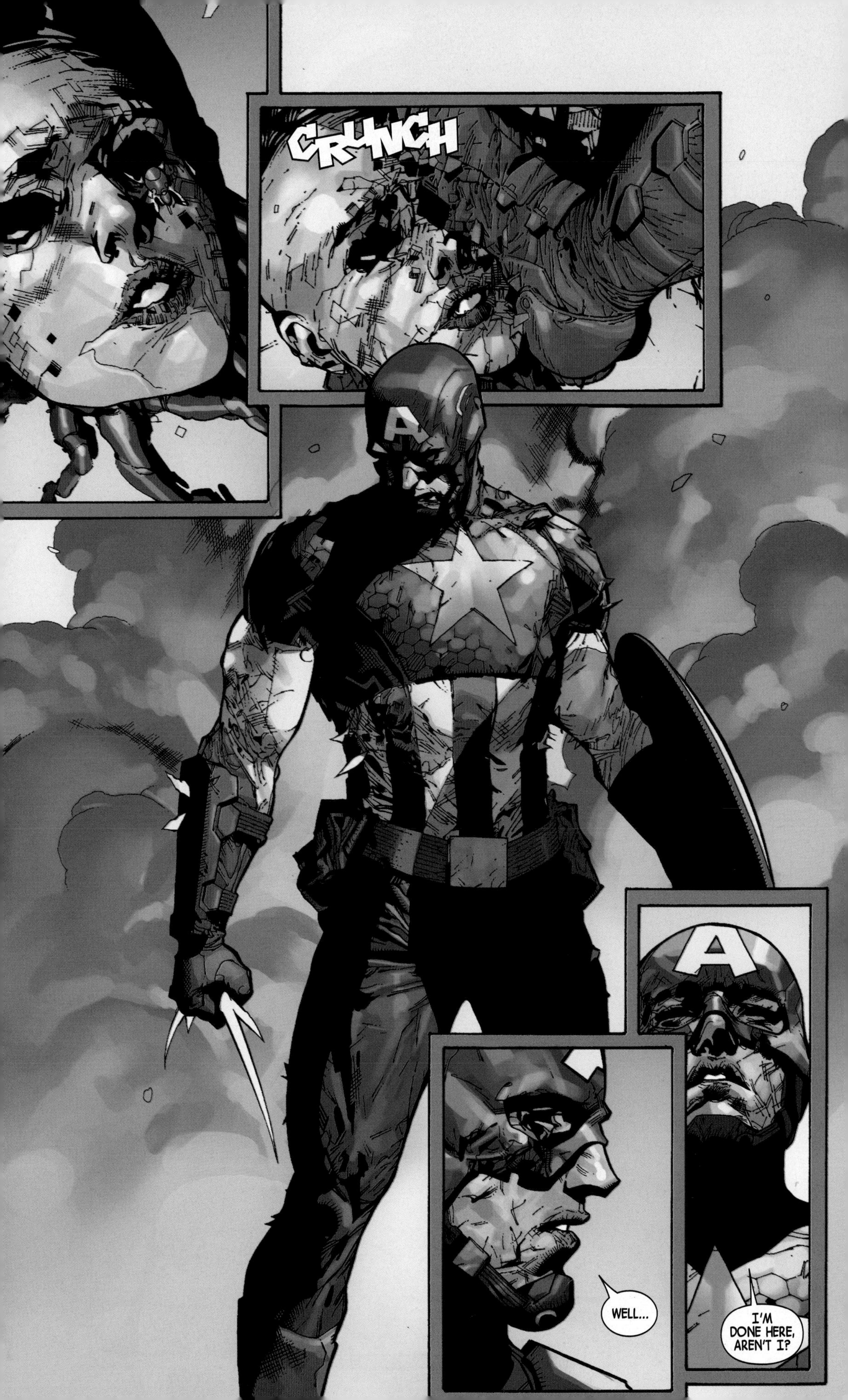
CRUNCH
WELL...
I'M DONE HERE, AREN'T I?

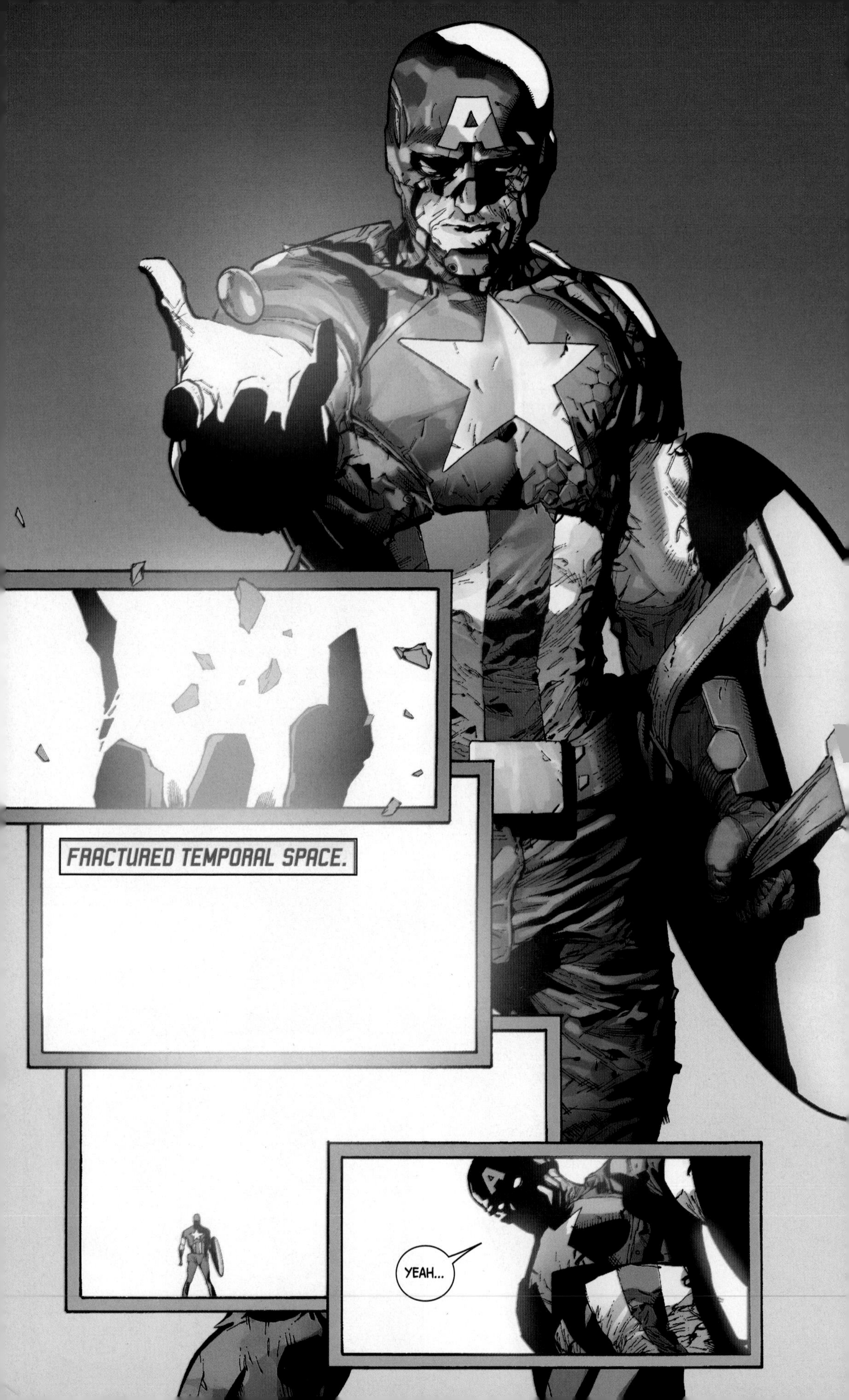
FRACTURED TEMPORAL SPACE.
YEAH...

"THE LAST AVENGER"

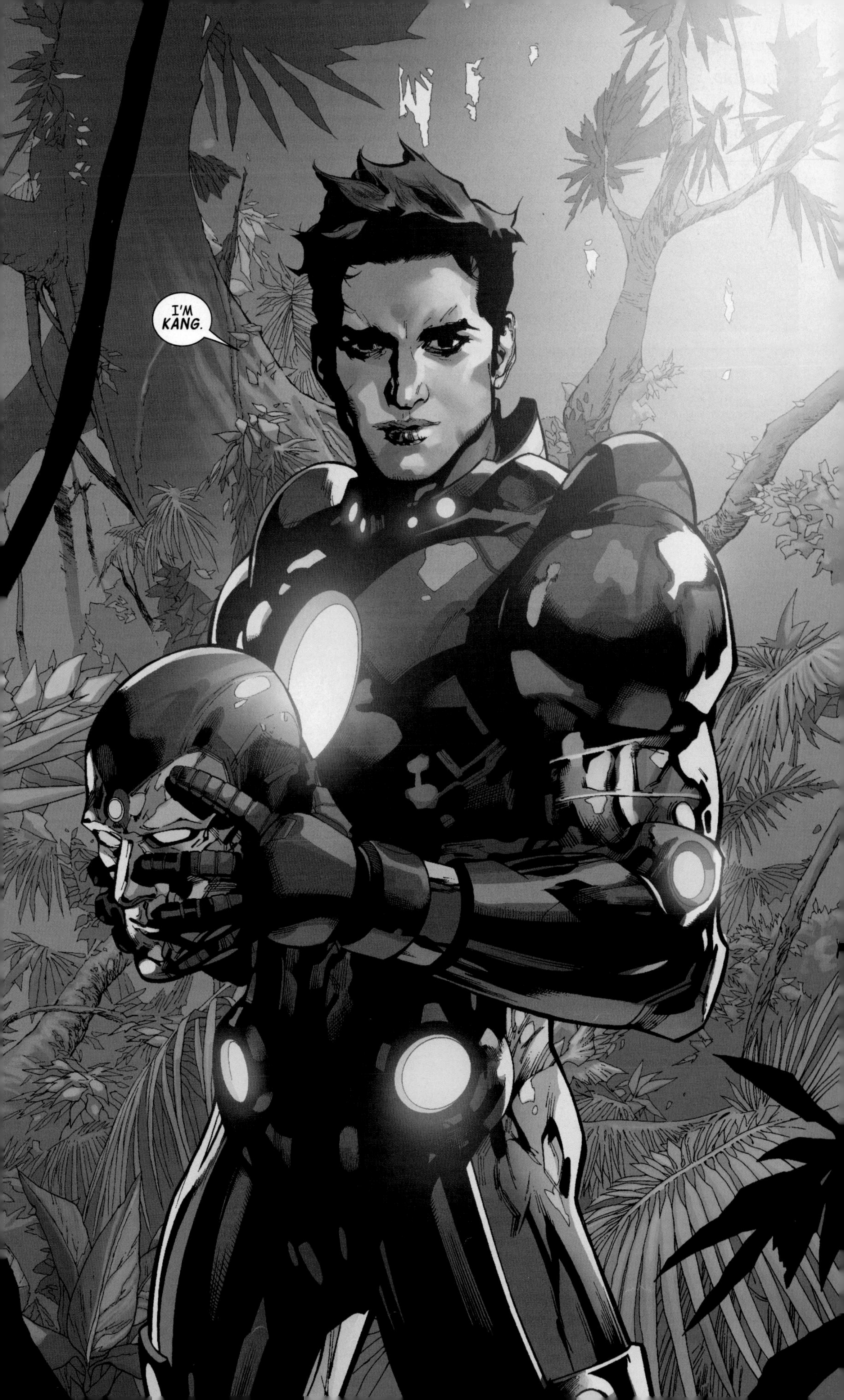
I'M KANG.

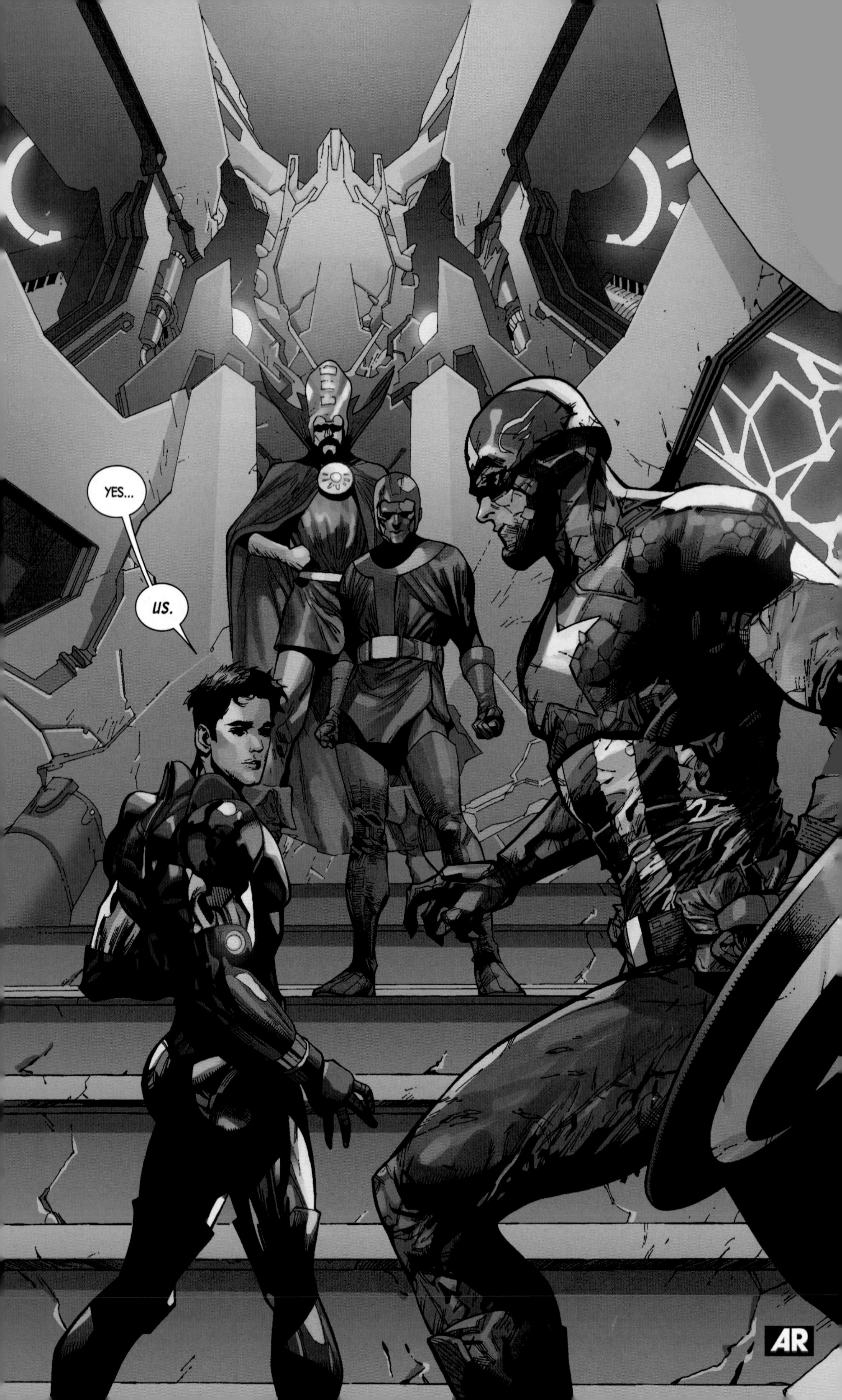
YES...
US.

IF YOU HAD ANY IDEA, NONE OF THIS WOULD BE NECESSARY.
YOU KNOW OF THE INCURSIONS. THAT THEY ARE RESULTING IN THE EARLY DEATHS OF UNIVERSES AND THEREFORE THE EARLY END OF THE MULTIVERSE...
YOU KNOW THIS BECAUSE YOU VERE ABLE TO STOP NE BY USING--AND SACRIFICING--THE INFINITY GEMS.
AND AS A RESULT OF THAT... THE TIME GEM WAS DESTROYED ACROSS ALL TIME...WHICH RESULTED IN YOUR LITTLE TRIP.
THESE ARE THE THINGS YOU KNOW.
"WHAT YOU MAY *NOT* KNOW IS THAT THIS--*ALL OF THIS*--HAS EVERYTHING TO DO WITH EARTH...IT HAS EVERYTHING TO DO WITH THE ILLUMINATI...
"AND IT HAS EVERYTHING TO DO WITH YOU."

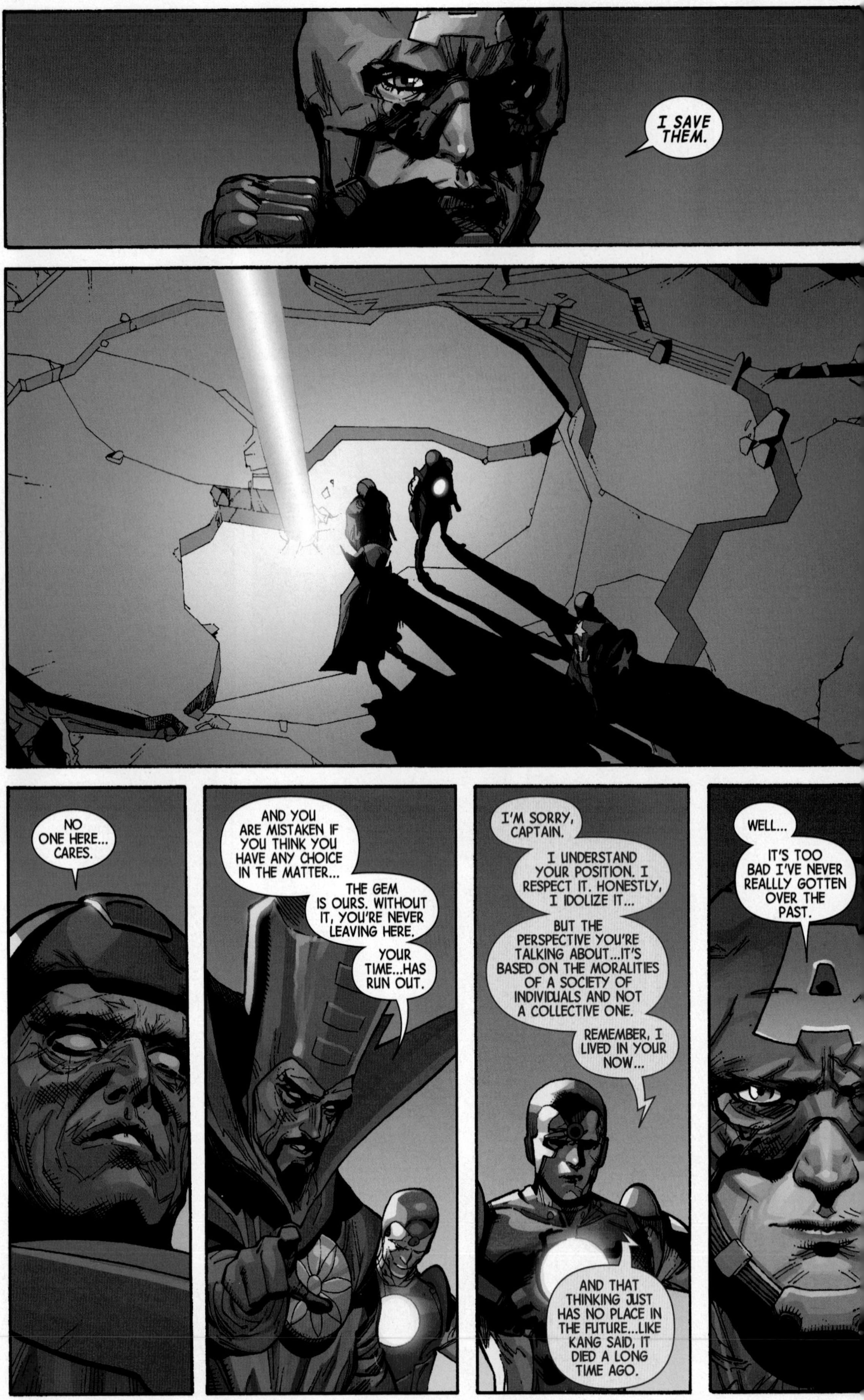
I SAVE THEM.
NO ONE HERE... CARES.
AND YOU ARE MISTAKEN IF YOU THINK YOU HAVE ANY CHOICE IN THE MATTER...
THE GEM IS OURS. WITHOUT IT, YOU'RE NEVER LEAVING HERE.
YOUR TIME...HAS RUN OUT.
I'M SORRY, CAPTAIN.
I UNDERSTAND YOUR POSITION. I RESPECT IT. HONESTLY, I IDOLIZE IT...
BUT THE PERSPECTIVE YOU'RE TALKING ABOUT...IT'S BASED ON THE MORALITIES OF A SOCIETY OF INDIVIDUALS AND NOT A COLLECTIVE ONE.
REMEMBER, I LIVED IN YOUR NOW...
AND THAT THINKING JUST HAS NO PLACE IN THE FUTURE...LIKE KANG SAID, IT DIED A LONG TIME AGO.
WELL...
IT'S TOO BAD I'VE NEVER REALLY GOTTEN OVER THE PAST.

NEXT: TIME RUNS OUT!

COVER GALLERY

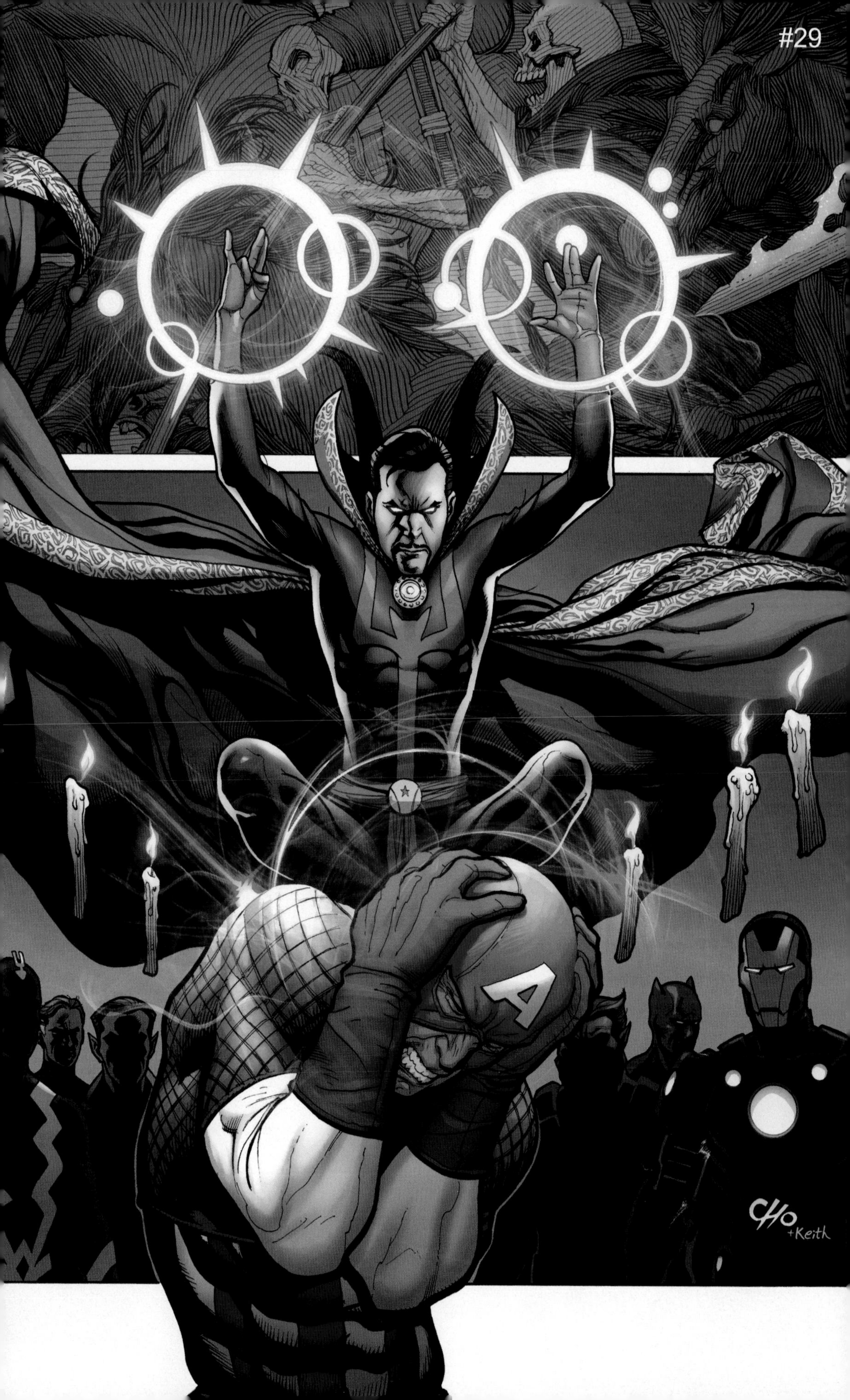
#29
CHO
+Keith

#30

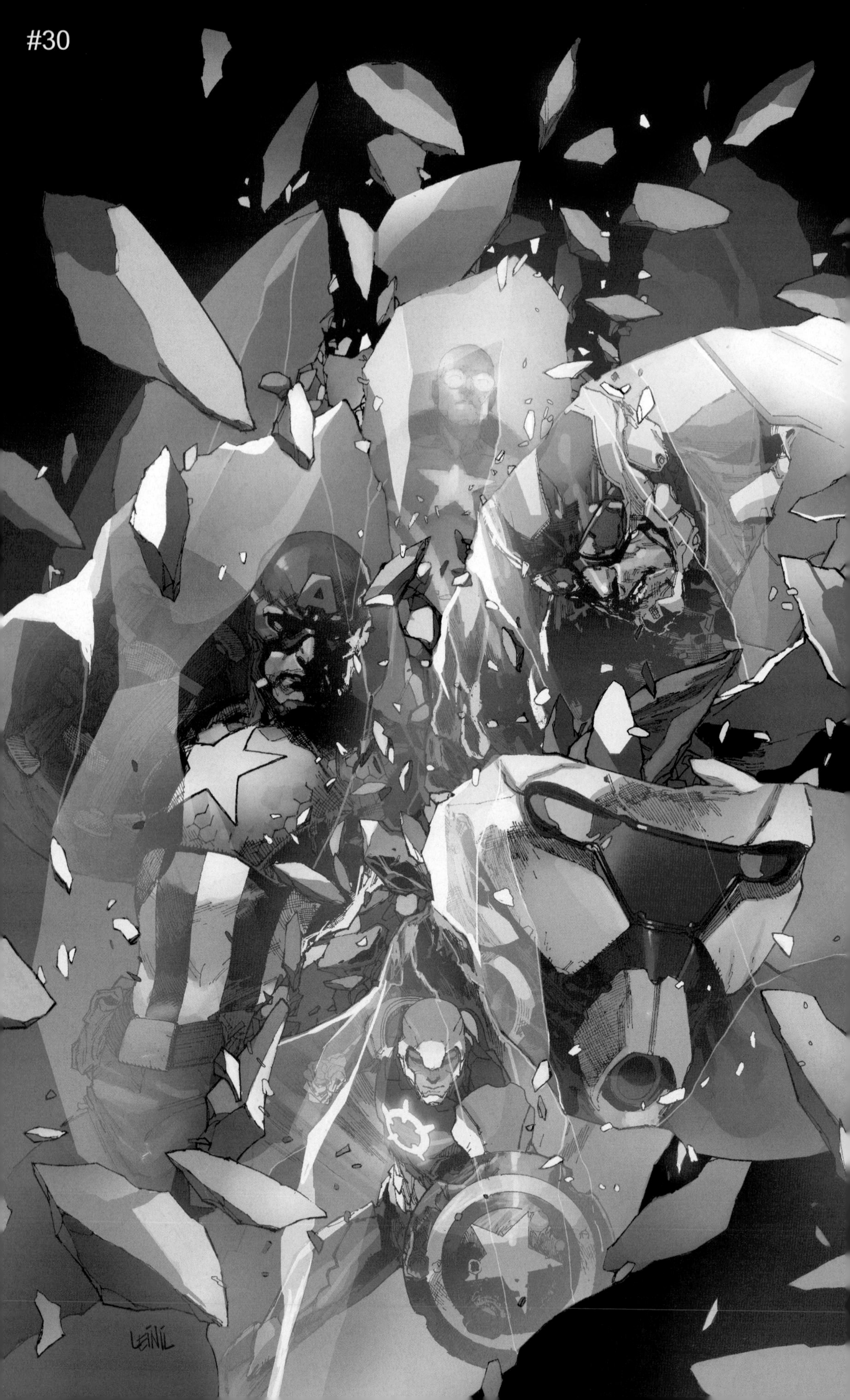
LEINIL

#30 VARIANT

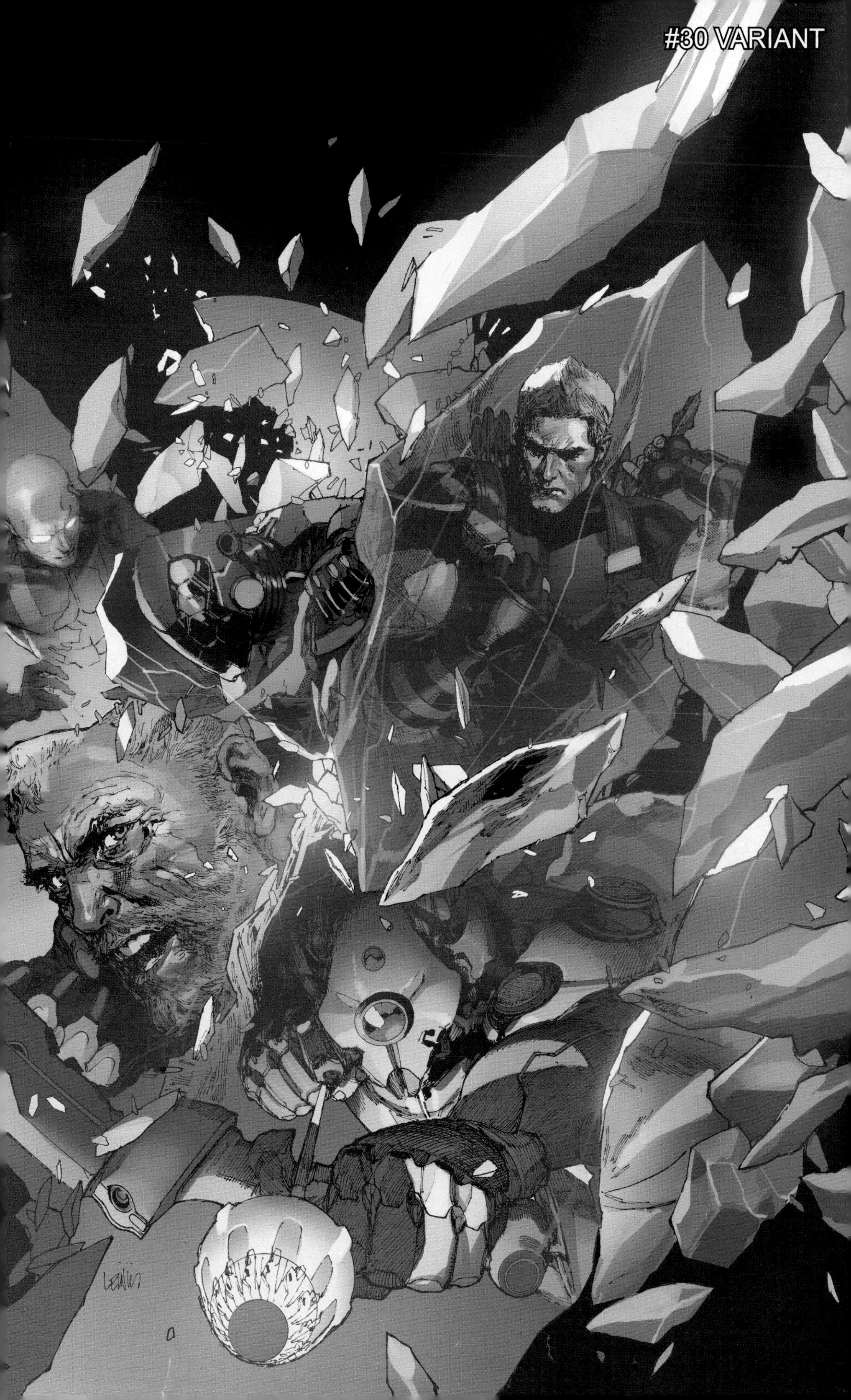

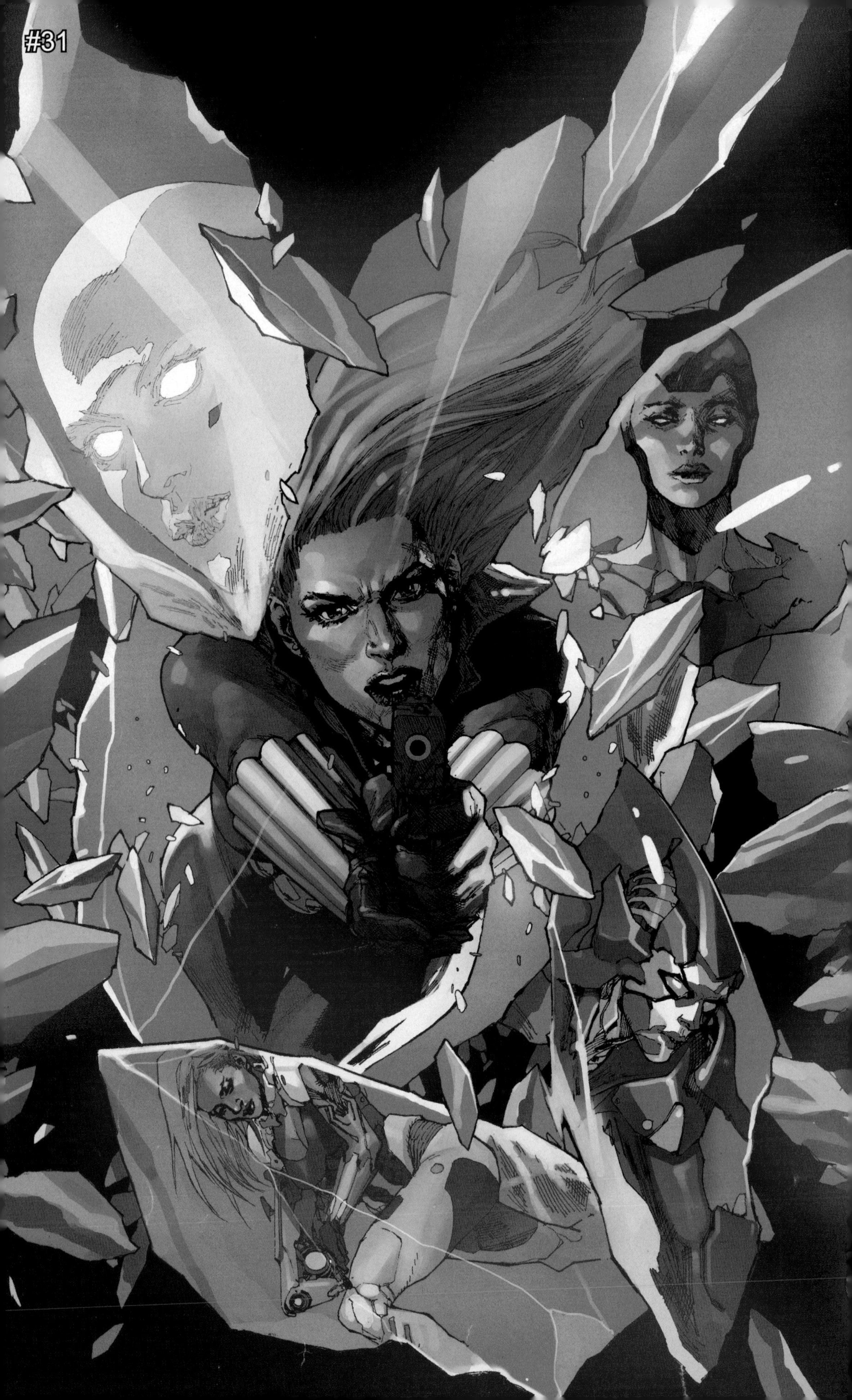
#31

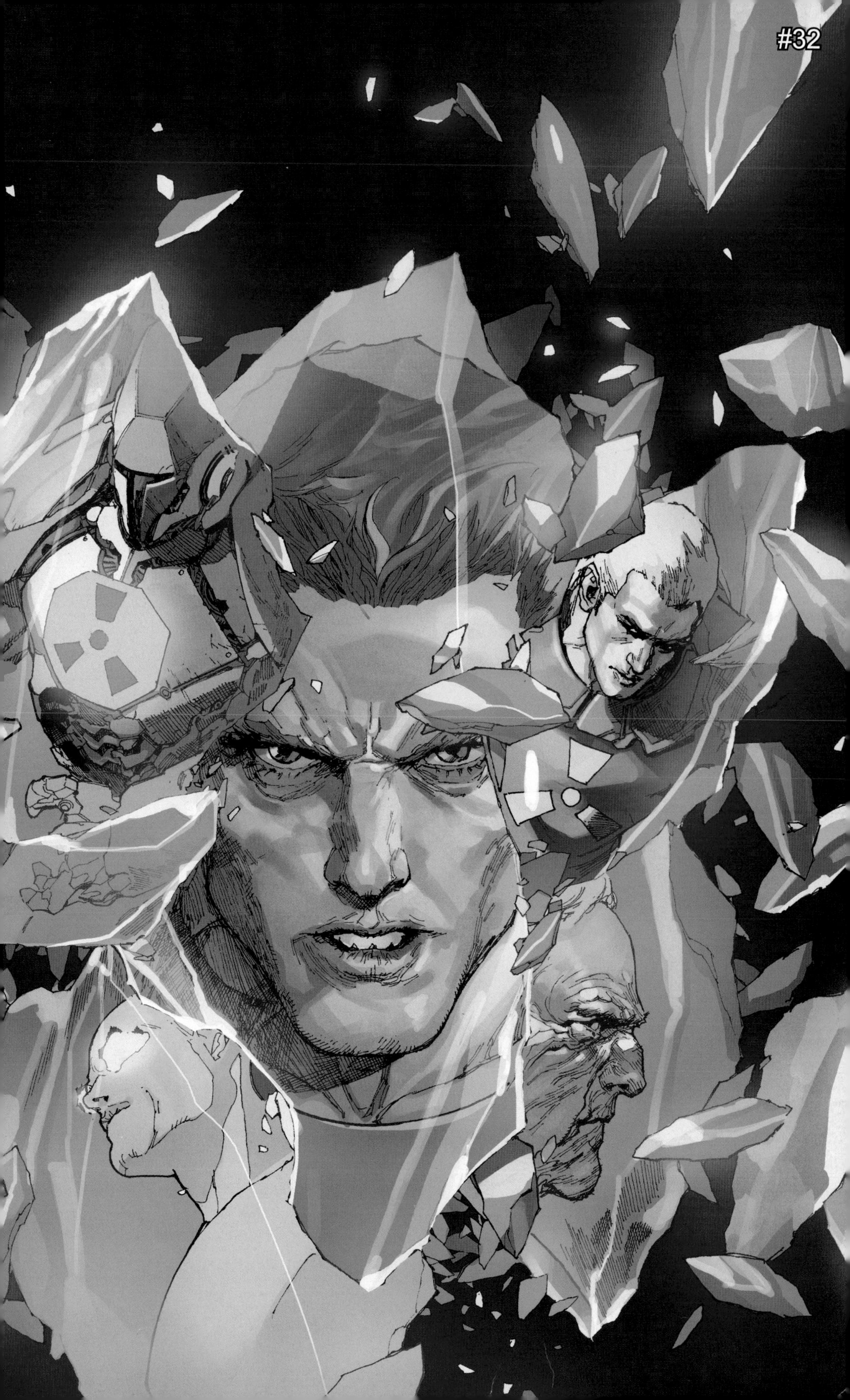
#32

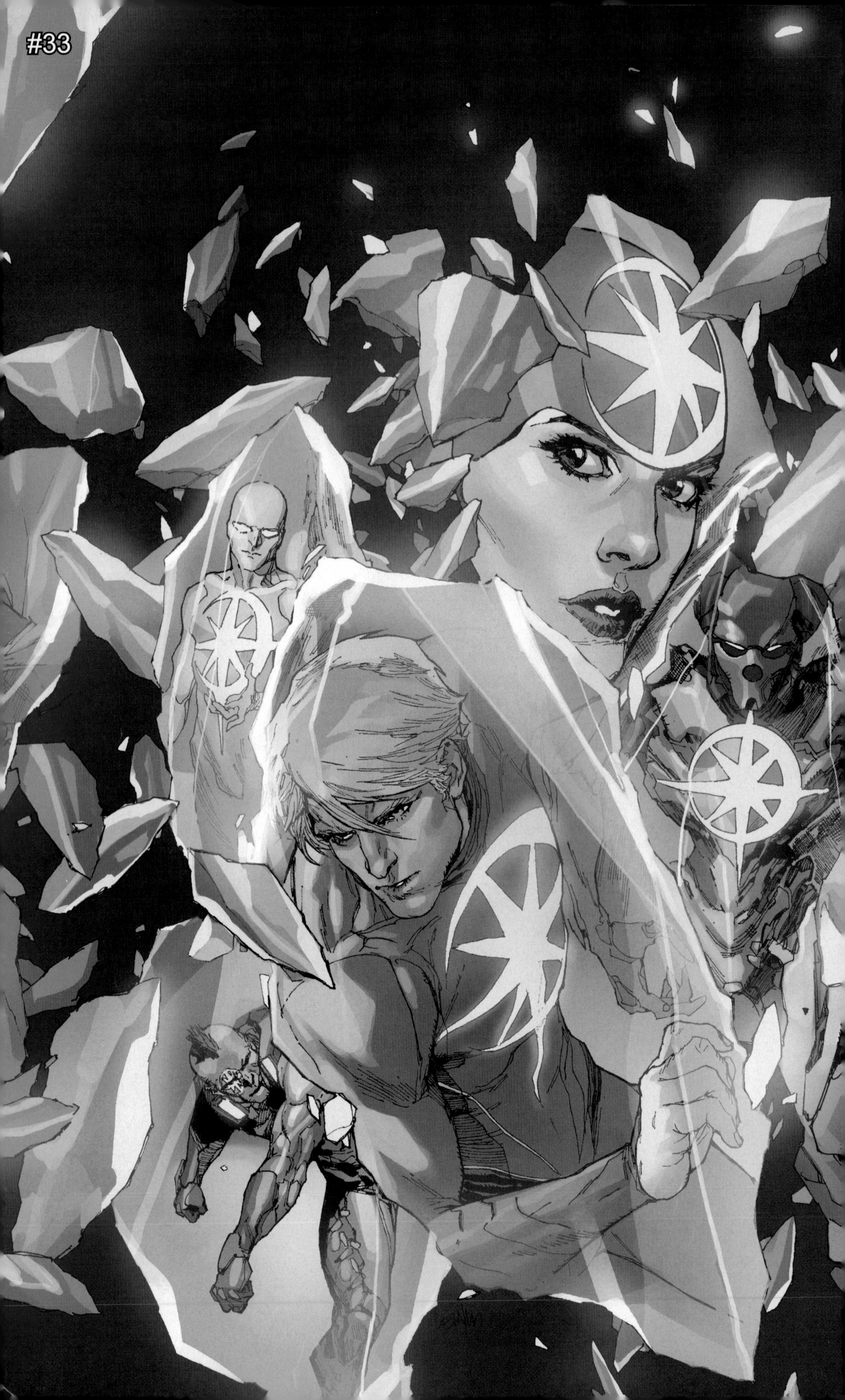
#33

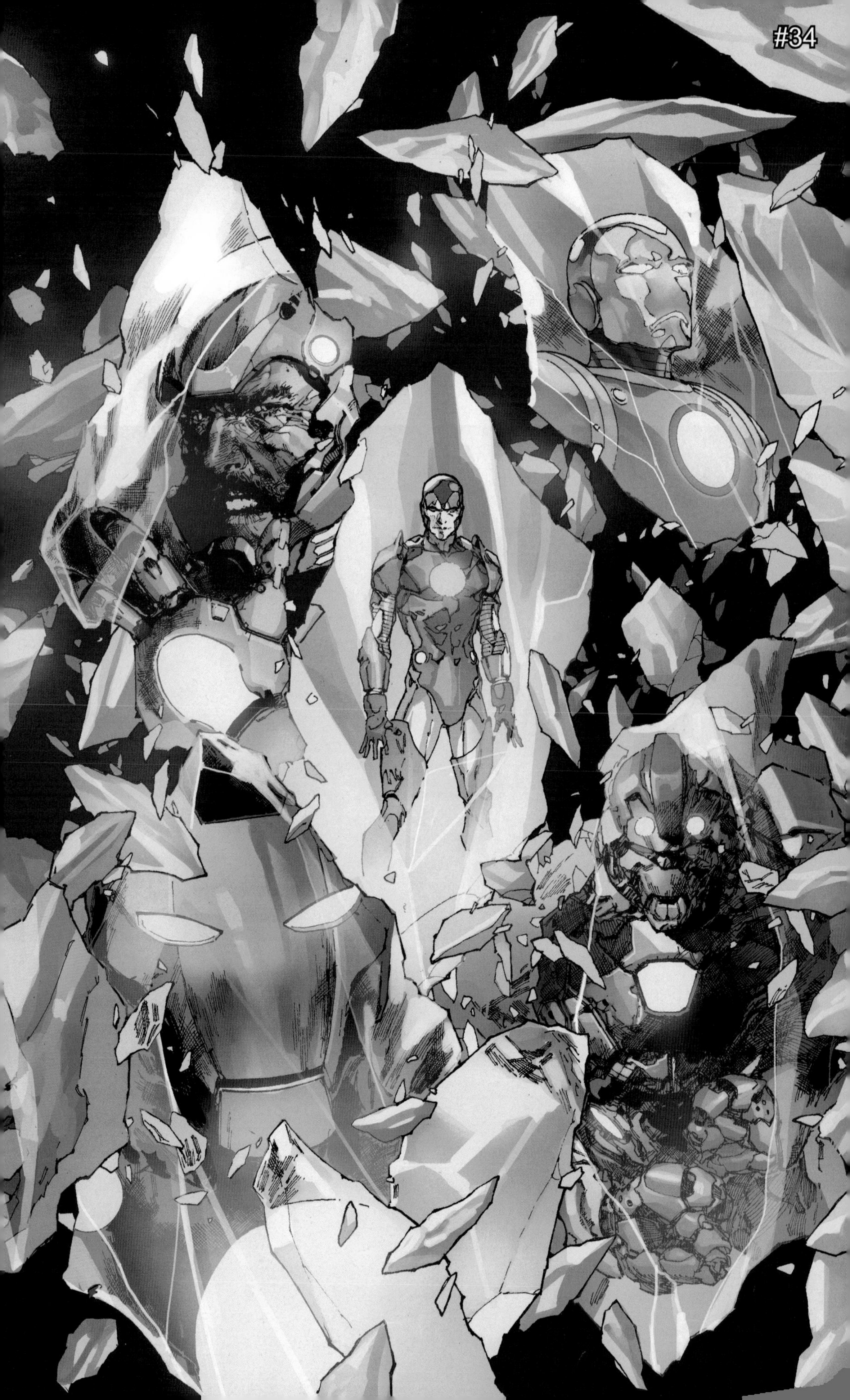
#34

#30-34 COMBINED COVERS

#32 GUARDIANS OF THE GALAXY VARIANT
BY PASQUAL FERRY & ANDY TROY

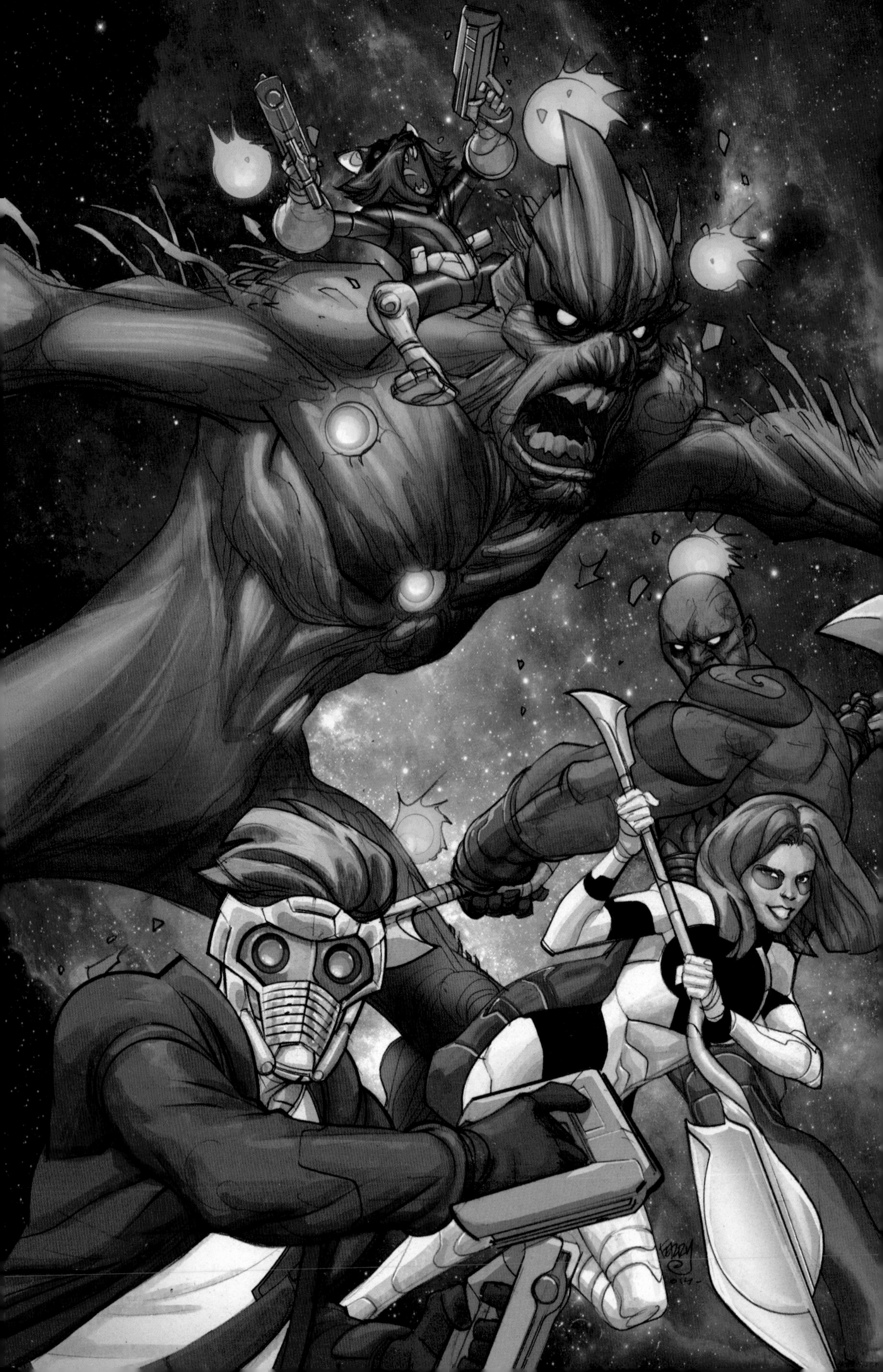